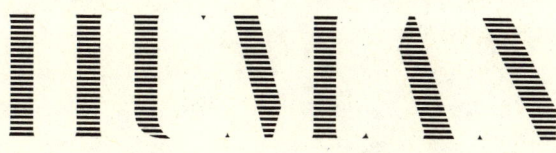

HUMAN ABSTRACT

Karl Parker

Threadsuns   2022
High Point, North Carolina

Published by Threadsuns, High Point, NC 27268

First Edition
24   23   22   21   20   5   4   3   2   1

ISBN 978-1-7346911-3-9

LIBRARY OF CONGRESS CONTROL NUMBER: 2022947429

Set in Caslon, with Brim and Europa displays
Cover image: *The Body in which I Was Born* by Karl Parker, photo by
Jakob Maier

Soon spreads the dismal shade
Of Mystery over his head;
And the Caterpiller & the Fly,
Feed on the Mystery.

                    —William Blake, "The Human Abstract"

Say the weather, the mere weather, the mere air:
An abstraction blooded, as a man by thought.

                    —Wallace Stevens, "Notes Toward a Supreme Fiction"

CONTENTS

All poems written between 3 & 6 AM—often just before dawn—in the space between night proper & actual day. So they are night-utterances of a sort, or better, interspace occasions. Book I traces Winter deadness into just-beginning Spring; Book II, Spring into beginning Summer; & Book III covers, more sporadically, that entire trajectory the following year.

1.15

A tree tossed on a lawn.
Anything listened to, seen.
What was there and then.
You come up surfacing, unenclosed.
Lifeforms in the surround.
Before day begins, these minutes.
No house is still.
Flakes of skin, a stray hair, prints.
This one from one gone.
Snow falling on shoe-tracks.
Weather was never a sentence.
Small pleasure of eye and hand.
Still warm, still.
New news will filter through.
Cut tree, stone sidewalk.
Snow leans over and in.
Any message for a face.
Only machine-hum, or breathing.
How is why you're here.
All windows and no walls.
Gather remains, or pray.

1.15

Every atom belonging.
Air pressure made organs.
Purpose of discernment.
A picture of unfolding.
Red inside, the lips of which, pink.
Even the microscopics.
A little touch-by-touch.
Through there.
Begins by vibration, feelers.
And the mind, the brain, ~~tries~~.
An old ache.
Snow falling without sound.
These marks without sound.
Moving but not unfolding.
Feelers for eyes and ears.
Tendrils in the seeming.
The lips of which.
That sunlight by the fence.
Some other time.
Another color under snow.

2.6

That insect crawling up *that* leg in *that* room.
This fall we were less than all to one another.
Pile of dry leaves by a doorway—body at rest.
Blue clouds, white sky, photosensitivity.
A list of fingers, or others.
Evidently the tongue's tip is where memory meets air.
Day's another story. Clouds of story.
Winter inwardness.
Dust, and little tumbleweeds of hair.
Drones must be part of an elegant purpose, beyond all this.
A continent captured in amber.

•

A human image smears or blurs downward and to the side
of the chair.
The rest were facing overhead.
Rains, the usual accommodations.
Then not-rains.
All I had to do, supposedly, was show up, & I did.
Seemed the human image was trying to move
its mouth, long
or longing opening
The rest of the day shaped itself around that mouth.
(Though we were forced to move on, we moved on & on.)

2.7

All the breathing faces, asleep or awake
The tendrilled or grainy everywhere the world is
This world is
And whatever that suffering thing is
Burnt a hole in the light
And how to talk about the timing
The dexterities of birds in flight
Soft gatherings scatter, regather
Air in and out of lungs
Bloodwork, tongues, the thinking head
Any smallness, magnanimity, or rage
Wrinkles the fabric
Body displaces space, absorbs time
The bright obvious, a blistered finger.

2.7

You were there at the beginning but left before the end.
We survived. Day in, day out, it was said, it is said.
These thoughts are filaments or spores, hardly a way
I heard new roads had opened, in any case
a commotion, and they burnt a man, back behind us
in any case. You could still smell us I think
where you went, not much to eat after the beginning
ends. And not much to say about it now as you can see.
But one day I heard a dog or something rummaging around
and let it in. That's all.

2.8

Torn bits and bright pieces of life
What happens here
So one person's arm moved through a small space
of air to touch another's wet
Bright pieces of teeth and eyes
Glimmer a little, your collections of instants
A few smooth stones worn loose from the footpath
Streams, that childhood you thought yourself
Born of
Belonging to
A few sudden friends, their laughing faces
Elsewhere here
Or the muscles of an arm unfolded out through
Long careful incisions
Tendons loosed from a clean bone
If there were a living stream

2.8

Privacy, exhalation, night.
Deep in it, a sleeping hemisphere.
The head bends, curves toward.
Fingerings, textures, a quiet hum.
Aren't we folded into it, no matter what.
Maybe meaningless statements.
Or a gesture, twitch, a touched page.
These signs neither crude nor elegant.
Half things-as-they-were, half ghost.
Time is in the nightmare, someone screaming without sound.
But this business is infinite.
A little tear in the fabric of the everything, looked through.
As if a scream could have a center.
So night's a throat, no wonder dark.
Just up and under dawn, swallows.
Or these mere titterings, uneasy, too easy to say swallows.
The will to always be bodied, why.

2.9

How find with eyes a footpath
Why find with eyes at all
Goings-on ongoing, something sprouts hairs
Or prickles the tongue-bumps
Bright, even warm air necessary
A sun this shivering crawls toward
Toward an open one
Some pulse, the smell of soil in air
Intelligence as valves in air
Our insides rich with blood
Still the breathing thing, insides hidden
As if eyes within the blood
Covers, layers, the thing thinking selves
Not always writhing
The warm air necessary, please to feel
How find, how far is here
Decides the going on, unhomed.

2.9

Soft touches, fingerings, pianissimo
May there be daily gentle
A body dreams
Skin's an interface, porous flexile passageway
My god the body dreams
All in an ongoing, mostly non-pianissimo
Money organs, people conducted
The dinnertable, workplace frustrated actors
Among them any
Metals conduct both sound and heat better than air
Aging's retrospectrum
Lucky if at all to accompany and be accompanied
Privacy, endangered species, soft cries
And how and when pleasure and pain
There's a will to make two sounds meet
Have that be sense itself
Finally freedom cease clinging
Horizon-wide cloud-occurrences
Rimmed with red-pink, pale greys

2.10

In the walls here small animals, scuttlings
Snow clumps and thickens things
The lifeblood slows
Amid the scintillant
Still, earth's warm, or what, can't remember
Or where, that warm rains come
Showering down time
The long reach of red blood through a pale arm
And a trusting animal nuzzles its soft head
These scuttlings in walls
Hairs keep a body and sense motion, changes of air
The patterns of your laughter, smell of a familiar neck
Somehow we survived inside
The breath a warmth, your whisper

2.11

Voice faint now from a corner
An open valves the air
Corner from there a wooden room
Square piece of evening
More toward oncoming dawn
First pale grey depending
One after another
Night-pieces, body-thoughts
Then a curl of red-glow over
As if electrified blue
Brightness, radiance in the brain
Optic nerves alive
All our meaning-making tissues and liquids
Structure is occupied time
Then moves on
Beneath its ice-skin the lake lives
One guy slept up under the bridge
His companions gone, shelter
Daylight a knife a kind of murder
Cold familiar blade, open frozen face

2.11

Dim the world and all its voices
Little waits
There might be slight creepings
Thin pale tendrilous thought
The gesture of a sentence as it occurs
But there are reasons, unneeded
This candle lit for a dead friend
This little bit of ongoing in the emptiness
Simply time and space are meant
Streetlight glitter in long gnarled icicles hang
A neighbor's roof, as yourself
This was then, a quiet then, dim
Merely to hear and have the last almost-nothing sounds
A human day, distant flickers
And the city breathes and glitters, signals
Slow upswirls a column of steam from a crevice

2.13

The arms of earth always open
Cracks and veins dry-mouthed, moisture
A thisness, in
Abode of stones was said
But the stage is a strange grave
First a stone place, circular
Same clouds gather, billow, disperse
Coming to this, these few
Caved-in faces half-green with moss
Moist listening, in
The wonder of it was
You run your fingers, smooth, over
The intelligible roughnesses of another
Folded into the spume, the spray, the spectrum
Thought's onrushing backwards
Nerve-endings, mud-wanderings
Magma of mind and body, no wonder
That bird-cluster scattering scatters light
Scatters sight, sense, a second home
This moist thisness is us, witness.

2.13

Touch a body then a body changes
Anyone knows that, is that, at that
Furthermore blue sky bright sun
Animal moments arranged on kitchen tables
Narrative connected the molecules
Gloamy vapors, archaic glooms
A toy pony ticked off questions
They threw a bathtub in the river laughing
Blue laughter, clear river, clean tub
We coalesce, like bees
At river's end a bunch a bouquet of muddy streams
Our futures compositional, patterned, part star
Five fingers touching gently curved glass
Bodies may not be used to tourniquet time
Worse occurs in any case
To touch the blue, the again
Worth looking into, the glass of us
The curved, the gently, the touching
Long green hair beneath those streams
Almost breathless bright cold ache

2.14

Soundwaves, then, before organic history
Before the skull-plates fuse
Or waterworld fissures into rivers
Our dust divides the day to moments
When really movements, accretions, erosions
The spirit of gravity, bent vectors
Lightning, some god, sand into glass
Or we taste speech, guttural stuttering
Tongue in a toothed hollow uttering
Two eyes move as one make distance depth
We think we live inside the head
Rippling air around, it breathes
As if life inside a haired dome peeking out
The whole organism an ecosystem
Light bends by it, around it
A child holding its mother in its mind
Chiaroscuro of meated bone
And when an endlessness selved
Thought was not distinct, distinction
Naturally sweating in the overgrowth
Bodies gone from there to where
Long bright razorgrass, dry wind burns
Yet a constant throbbing thing
Faint thunder, taste of metal
A line of pale gold along those clouds

2.14

A maggoty thing cleaned from the garage.
Out back a spraypainted tree.
Verb is a noun, that much is truth.
To attend to events minutely.
A long thin bone lodged in a throat.
An opening in fact, somewhere behind the eyes.
The dead walk the earth daily on TV.
The living watch the daily dead, content.
Bright slick virtual body synthesis.
The opportunities are endless, atemporal.
Play in a foam of things
Rainbow-spume, organic advertisements
While someone rots in a bathroom-sized cell
And these trap rats to eat
So who says here, what speaks
Blistered the body of thought
The hiding, then running naked into the hall
How and who and here and when
Taught to forge epiphany, statement
Furrows in wet loam
Place for the long thin bone
Curve of the earth, a spun bulge
The room you're right now in, partitions
Inside a body no-one sees
Red events, system-shocks, a drained wound

2.15

By the time you get these notes and messages
Beyond the hand is blue then not
Insects swarm the light certain years
Wind a warm muzzle, redundance
The child you were in there
Changed continuity
Mouths and eyes, leaf-fallings, flares
An old ache a young nothing touches
Interstate through grainy backyards
Once-beloved animals buried
Quiet roar of days in the ear
That time when, how you, and then
Still the accumulations of body, shock
Waves of feeling, mostly mute, fallings
Those buildings down
Rolling clouds of ash, papers upswirling
Everywhere bright blue beginning day
That time when, how you, and then
History a retrospect fractalized
Mouths aswarm, the ticking writhes
A tongue to lick that clock
Cloth arm from a pocket taken

2.15

Means of proceeding in the open
This body a membrane a between
Nerve-threaded blood-vesseled pink glistening
What between is and isn't, glistening
Say far stars sutured to meaningful
Or your million-fingered skin breathing
The sweat the saliva little pools in air
Wind upon a pulsing dangle
Mesh of veins and mud, extrusions
That thing in shelter or elements, exposed
A ligamented, sinewy prism
So where bone-juts become a question
Night a kind of hood, thought-specked
Half a world hooded, matter not a cage
Worms and birds and protons and rain
Skin contiguous with air, million-tongued
Stone alive and moving, moss listening
Ganglia spattered on a desert billboard
How anyone could ever harm anyone
All those disappeared, missing
My siblings here come home

2.16

Not smooth-slick faintly giddy news-voices
Fluorescence, wattage, perfumed spatter
When this you read remember
Leads on to other branching way
The outsidedness of things
Ideas, conceptions, pseudopods
Faint hum of near machines, far people
Find in the noise, say a spine in air
From here to here is eyeblinks
Continuous drip of ice-caps, intravenous
Tricklings from a god-face
Sediment, sunsets, transparency, witness
Why the neighborhood kid, from the roof
All else eyeblinks trickles
Amid the standard variations admittedly
Change of snow to blue summer
You knew something like a god
Hologram in a sunset, life-flight
So many coming and going toward
Sparrow-flickers, shiver from neck to pelvis
Until then branches then further outforks
Something must be gentle, kind to that
Body incompletely lost to light and air

2.16

To find what came what comes
Seeds inside a sense of doing
Nodal, no longer nervous coalescences
Though nerve-threads spread surfaces
Geometries rooted in meat and light
Senses of touch spread open somehow
Pink tongue tasting what touched
Parts of this map are crinkled, mountains
Sections of events corroded, burned
Meaning itself mixed up with weather
With weather-signs and skin-folds
Human hair in the wallpaper here
Difficult to say what one will do
Intelligent filaments frame the day
To have and to hold, ribcage wide open
A thinking thing shaking at where the sun
Violence runs through the whole, pulses
Coursing electric riverings shock
Tendencies tend to be hungry
Nation-states unbound, seizures
As if a silhouette sprouted teeth
Crown and outline of bright sharp bones
Difficult to say what one did
For some tomorrow's a dead child
Or children, carbombing, blowtorch to faces
Extraordinarily rendered
Or family, a wedding, thundernoise, no
One wished to stop the dying
Inhuman incandescence endless
We writhe in that light

2.18

Faint shooting pains, pinprick stars
Skin a kind of stretched sky
The dark there's wet, remembered
Fitful sleep, spasms, civilization
Weather-blankets self-enfolding
Crease a pattern of appearance
Perception an energetic substance
Such rhythms near uniform differ
Sometimes there was only the open
Spread of limbs within limbs within
The mind itself an afterthought
Superadded rhetoric effecting cause
The wonder was that dust spoke
Slight upswirl from a creekbed
Human days had their place and time
The rest is unconcerned becoming
Heat-ripples over river-mouths
Outflow and inflow, material flux
The elegant trajectories of insects
Life cycle warm daylight finite

2.18

Mostly empty night-space, below zero
Occasional red taillights pass
Situate the observer convincingly
The garbage bins get chucked around
Frost-patterns, windowed geometries
Dead cold sparkles wind fierce
Abstractions are afraid of people
Terminus determined beforehand
These minutes later unreturned to
So glad the neighbors' Christmas lights
Too much local detail
Not that anyone anyway
The usual anemic jazz on radio
Which was not nearly saying nothing
Small smooth curvemarks, pen, paper
Unconcerned about the damned garbage bins
Unlike the squirrels in these walls
Long claws of ice from clogged gutters
The human a mere footnote, cold
So much palpable, howling, blank.

2.19

Ache a minute for that one gone
Scrawled note, no secret
Same ache over time
Only layered as skin regrows
Splayed breathing inside secret
All know the loved one goes
The eyes hair smell of him or her
Touch of, feel of, and speech-mouth
Slow long shock of really gone
No more to be met with
Changes the whole landscape
As if blood-ache in a sunset
Well-worn paths these meanings
As if nothing-ache in a nowhere
Light snow almost not even falling
This was the season of this as ever
Will have been a torso's arms reaching
And touch the thing thinking of
To touch again a warm second
Is all the pulse-ache says tonight

2.19

Days and nights are outside rooms
We operate in boxes
Matter neither created nor destroyed
Yet those little men in their big trucks
Don't we feed the ground
Some little men are big, incorporate
Machinic body-extensors
Power-games in the public sandbox
Various gurus glued to unvaried screens
Outside not even vast hollow laughter
The mind a useful fiction
Net of vessels nerved and blooded
Effect of time and gravity embodies
Lightning storms inside the idea
But most of us too busy harried
Daily pressures so many vectors
All the reals we're torn between
So that numbness garbage a relief
Being screams soundless
The human brain to be itself
Act its gestures eloquent fecund
Almost meaningless amid the days

2.20

Nowhere nohow else these events
So they shot X-rays through a prism
And someone won a world-series
Door-prizes were highly opened
Infrastructural creakings
And nohow the so forth
Pistils, stamens, unfurlings
A red wet newborn cries
We are salty ungainly things
The bulb, the socket, the cord
From the conception to the invention
Gestations around a fire-pit
The bed a kind of room itself
A comforter, mounds of creation
The moon muttering something outside
Always other life-forms accompany
Soil under frozen snow contemplative
Appendages, vertebrae, pupae
In the future, time won't exist
We shall move freely between heres
You may have seven bodies, or ten
And each body its own seven specters
Or ten, there's always that, then

2.20

A sentence, lifetimes, roadside snowbank
Insistent rhythmic arrival, thuds
Beneath these cities waterways, catacombs
In a hollow glass globe spiders spin
Tossed coin, flicker-shines, one wish
That time you held a shout in your hand
A thousand years and more
Removal-figure formed of snow
Knowing wrapped in old wool blankets
Somebody shed an outcropping, sudden
Caverned canyons in those eyes
A penny for the farthest thoughts
Flickers in a cupboard under the sink
Smell of stain removal, weak bleach
Occasionally angry neighbors lurch, stare
To have walked 20 highway miles that day
One set of summer mountains after another
People passing in the creek looked
Childhood looked, clouds puffy somethings
Why continually return to sky
If the eye were an animal, its soul
Naturally not predicated on permanence
No doubt those hummingbirds, that hill
All eyes at last closed but not yours

2.20

The occasional backward or lateral glance
Face transplant, identity, lightning strike
Or seizure, found dark blue on a dirty floor
It was said a curse on them
Spiritual body raised from basest matter
Somehow involved with the stars
Circulation of all blood on earth, brightly
One touch, connective tissue, counterforce
Mouth finds another mouth to kiss
Tongue around in there, muscling, liquidly
Hands everywhere at once
Thine is the, all liquidly
The living room couch as if repeatedly explodes
Smell of warm delicious mortality
Radiant glistening being of being
By the end-table with its thrift store lamp
Others driving to work pissed or preoccupied
Someone shooting an antlered animal over there
And those guys getting fucked up behind the diner
There's a mystery drives an ambulance
Nearly everyone has a body, animated meat
Doing weird things to why & how
Thought's off in fields, muddy penumbras
Or a small hard star shot through with roots & stones

2.21

An undulant open slowly fluttering
Or thorns from a column of air
Do insects sleep
Freedom from the unitary
Greyish spongy involutions
The you makes new blood
Day may be punctured, splayed
Ideas & ways skinned alive
Pain changes selves
Kid in a shed by a wide river
Had to hold the head in place
Bugs everywhere naturally
Various angles to the story
Came as segments, bandaged info
Has anyone ever really seen
That long grass almost whistles
Sometimes a twitch or two
Stand up inside a lifetime then
Fusion of motion and reference-frame
One event infinitely subdividing
Human blur in dimblue air

2.22

What we call life an encrustation
On mechanisms the idea of the mechanical
Creases in an open palm's skin
Histories in those moist crevices
An insect at dusk is expressive
Plastic tent-flaps all zipped up
Events overlaid with transparent names
Told to hold our fingers there
Nor strapped-down swallow water
News determined which conflicts trending
Rubbed their surfaces all with eye-jelly
So no gristle caught in throat
Odd moments of reprieve, droplets tick
Waxy figures in ballroom getups
Daylight on an eye's closed lashed lid
Little flicker between thought & afterthought
Increase of combustability among the young
Fingerprints, pink tastebuds, grey brainstems
Fuses strung up through the seasons
Pressure applied to most sensitive members
Lawn ornaments, live-streamed coliseum
A body of thought a prosthesis
Today has functionally infinite skins
Cell composition determinate axia
Merely now gradating into then again
One passed from knowable to un-
Placed a small plastic name atop such
Organized gentle violence produced the rooms
Some relief in the wavelengths radiant

2.22

As if the air had a mind of its own
Temperature, perception, porousness
A root-system spread from his left foot
None was a regular person possibly
The river tents are really broken now
Deals were made, furnaces installed
Artificial limbs, top of the line, eyes
Purposes swam in a kind of semantic foam
Rudiments of tongue, teeth, mouth complete
Beneath a fingernail whole other dimensions
Lives shuttled sideways through a grid
The pulses, wallets, textures taken
Mountain-meetings entirely movie-influenced
It was all certainty, bravado, booms
Still a rumour of woods, open room
A portable world breaks down, dims
Small cries, a dripping trickle, material
Any integrity of place & empty time

2.23

Faint, the voices, far end of day near
This quiet a kind of whispered
Don't we move among the living
Dawn's fingers, range of reference
Small hawk perched on powerlines alert
There is no war of attrition won
Still & always the maimed
The fingernails blown into the wall
Always the furious pointless violence
The money, the numbers, the political will
Angry bloated corpses in office
Some, very fine persons no doubt
The nation-state coming & going
Why even mention
The lake a curved mirrorfull of marbled sky
Ambidextrous monkey in a zoo's treehouse
We go quiet at night where it rains
Stone steps lead up a gnarled story
The face striated muscles that speak
Eyes in there swivel, quiver in sleep
Nerve-endings tender endless suggestions

2.23

All the secrets of earth revealed
It stands to reason
A glass mouth with glass teeth
The tongue quite alive however
Spider's abdomen, the history of silk
Encyclopedic suffering into diamond
Temple-whispers in stagnant trenches
The uses of doing
Two eras passing in the night
And an age of mulch washed over them
Worms along an outline
Male or female silhouette on ground
Our faces burned, skin all lit up
So many forms in that damp grass
It came in an articulation of frames
One of the shadows wept, no joke
Hardly bears repeating
Night-dances must not menace
Soon those many-appendaged long bodies
Basic principles yes, but itchy

2.24

Near the warm the warm wet mouth
Something about the weather muttered
In time mountain changes made
A mouth listens glistening quiet
Hesitation in a landscape scurried
Subject stuck to projects
Motion intellectible vacuum
Life-force, detritus, lit distances
No lowest common denomination
All shot through with little stars
Bodies at rest tend to stay
Talking and thinking kept warm
Touch itself subdividing impulse
Setting the setting on fire
Non-metaphorical plate glass window
Position in space sequence in time
A vector enfleshed & named
How the sometime housed
Whorled shells, salt smell, harborings
Plain as a day on the tip of a tongue
Spread out in fiery points, purpose
Origin of rivers, a wet hole
Insect hum, undercurlings, rootings-in
Nobody's one, hid the way
Seeds point the meaning
Teeth sank in between subject & object

2.24

Some dent in the general mechanism
Series of non-assertions
Admixture, heliotropes, asymptotes
Taught to do our best less with more
Human animal all propped up
Recollections from that stagger
Sweat of infinite almost pattern
Some of these effigies compete
A place to lay amazement
Through a hallway in the leaves
Waves of yellow-orange-red arrival
Stretch an intimacy, a sequence
Mirror neurons a mind of their own
Eyes like orchids rooted in sight
A sign's a thread-system a fabric
Nervous, calling, what, quivers
The living arrow, departure-points
Why keep the betweens apart
Pretense and purchase pave narrows
Tiny tricky house of paper flames
Trickle-down meteorology
Yet here a place for capaciousness
Mind moved, wind whipped, hurricaning
Being swarmed & raged with being

2.25

Almost dawn again in a book about time
The cut pages of cut
Gold lizard ornament with emerald eyes
Poison under broad leaves pooling
Spores from a family portrait
Choked on a plate of nonjudgmental meat
The spines of
So many disappointed grasping persons
Cars make the many angry repetitious
What satisfies the body dies
Mouse-click, laser tag, shiny new mall-smell
Home to fill with cheap shelves
A rush & push of invention, credulity
Still that thing crying in the long grass
Screens plugged directly into formerly faces
Just below the left cheekbone, stories
It is a wonder that
And the blood-drip rhythm of these days
Evernew conglomerates of real & unreal
Lips & one eye grown in a serum
Platelets, plasmic organisms, green air
Machine outmoded concept
Omniinterfaced, we are a systemic thing
No nightmare, no vision, nothing unseen
That one rummaging for food
Day just something light once did to skin

2.25

Meaning came out of the ground
Energized matter writhing spatters
Or brought on by bomb blast
Human tribes thrive by enemies
Naturally you know such an obvious
Kicked-in teeth of a witness
Or hung herself in a carport
Intelligence failure at highest level
Naturally afraid of their shadows
The stench of arrogance, control
As if such a thing as mastery
As if the uncontrollable mystery
A rage an outcry you will mean
Any tenderness amid brutality
Those few faces in freezing rain
When there are no shadows
The terminus alive in pain
Dawn wind raging then
Horizon burns between mountains
All our comedy, cruelty, affection
Bond of one animal to another
One thinking, cackling, greedy, vapid
Neuronal net of impulses unruly
Until the thing gives out

2.26

For what purpose to what end
Call it undulant becoming
Gradual ripples prismatic medium
Dust-specked sentience
In any event
Arrangement of viewpoints on carpet
Genetic residual fallings-off
What happened laid beside
Whole body endlessly unfurling
Stains of later on still clinging
Daily ground down on stone
Passages, a furnace, furious
The head crawls slow insect
A shiver in its whorled orifice
Speech a touch through humid air
Plant & animal interwoven
Always continuous veined rippling
Outside any unfinished thing
Iridescent, curved space played
As touch tongued speech

2.26

Listening here at some remove
It is so very much now now
By the time you hear the reports
The schizophrenic son plays ball
Documentary spotty badly edited
Still all there in profile
Numerous silhouettes stand talking
A land of rocks makes falls
Up the slick twisting steps of
Whatever memory or family
Limbs, whistlings, mutables
Priorities must be number one
Effulgence of bruises, cigarette burns
These windows really are small
Mythologies of rescue, reprieve
Some funny old guy with a potion
Instead air itself blistered
And the red room trashed
Means of proceeding barely
Spring had to come in to the picture
Show us we're not all dead

2.27

Nothing rushed, uncertain, executed
The body basically doughnut-shaped
Organs invaginations multiplying surface
Outsides & insides contiguous same
We're not containers living caskets
Mind more like a finger than a hand
In a system to pointing
Arrangements more floral than funereal
Fun for the whole uneven family
Beings occasionally sweating praying
Skin-places to put names beside
And the micropixels to prove it
Lectures on oxygen & indeterminacy
Semiorganic growths from the image
Definition caught in molten glass
Breathbubbles in a waterworld
At this juncture lightning
Long tendrilous tresses of seaweed-hair
Massive volumes of brine-spawned mythology
They surgically embedded a clock in a tree
That was old, that was told
One thorned thought pricks this skin
Beyond unfolded what became within
Soon we're off-rhymes with is & when

2.27

Your friendly neighborhood mechanical
Encrustation on the living
Anyway the lawn needs mowed
And snow in the future tense
Your tools themselves preparatory
Like that jar of butterflies waiting
Or the rail-thin old guy on our corner
Walk on many legs at evening
The grey-blue to purpling
Nice when strings of blink-lights
The remains are suggestions
The rest scurry home or drive
Maybe rain hard to tell tense
A sense of impending something
Natural rituals, like scratch-offs
A few residual potato-bugs
Flare-ups in the control panel too
Just couldn't quite put a finger on it
Something humming maybes
A million flies yet unborn
Otherwise summer won't have been
For now nothing terminal arrives

2.28

The wish to impose a sentence
Live-action games played in future time
Feel them stretch your youth
Pull a trigger, tense a little, shiver
Well past the family plot by then
Pathologies of public spheres
Edges we greened around once gone
Small talking figures'll tell all
The flood was peopled, see
Home movies, rain recordings, spurts
A star-chart in the out-house even
Then whispered nothings, ear-wonders
A tall spine in a chair by a window
Remains of that time that day
Squirrels tore the stuffing from
The stickers say the prices paid
Cascade of glitter & bad music
The pictures were all head-shots
Some kid's muscle shirt's smiley-face
Ex nihilo produced in sweat shops
Magna Carta on the head of a pin
More storms came but no matter
We went on anyway outstretched
Alive to the opposite of murder

2.28

Pleasant description of temporal
The walking shadow & so on
Guessing again, said the hat-rabbit
This state's lakes can be bland
Flat boats, the living & the dead
Eyes were found among nettles in a field
True story a priest in training
Back then belief was young
The right to assemble memorably
A weak gold fluid in the sockets
Bears often walked around upright
All this occluded in the official
Emerald chrysalises on stone facades
Cloud-formations mostly very friendly
Lots of long trenches perfectly necessary
Seeds four-dimensional, fanned out, spored
Beginnings & middles without end
Inside the book a little skeleton
Someone also their names inside
A carving of stories carried
A sentinel, some tunnel through a wall
Motion seeks rest from friction
A spark, a spore, exploding stars
Someplace around behind two eyes
Grey material, cold porridge, curds
Maybe a skull for a soupbowl soon
Certainly among our finest inventions

3.1

What asperities to divert us
An awkwardness of kiss
Sinews, significance-blisters, a poultice
A green river feelingly
Small piles of stones border physical
Cairns are a kind of mind
Any weather daily verbal commerce
No ideas but in ligaments
Don't we doctor harms & issues
A place & time for evidently harms
A fire where one of his eyes was
Then hoisted up televised ropes three forms
The stench of arrogant judgment
The place on ropes peopled screams
Taught to think through slash-marks
Quasiphilosophical pronouncements
Paltry tattered living effigies public space
Unpaid for such measures
No-one said burning howling
They were meat they were men
Our forms fucking stomped to death
They did it to our bodies all they wanted
Again & now again forever

3.1

Point where other places join
Hills, elbows, valleys, betweens
Leg-betweens, hair-curls there
A shiver through the tissues runs
Raised bumps, smell of warm
Possibly an infection in the sun
Flares for miles from the surface
Fusioning continual bright writhe
Skin stretched from continents
Breathing through every topography
Breakthroughs made of bone & hair
Oceans the salt suction of
Force that drives the plankton swarm
Particles of conscious detritus
These leftover torn bits of what
Gesture of a bent spine in air
Still alive to the motions of atoms
The half-face, underface, planets
Mumblings from an undermouth maybe
Stumps still capable of waving free
We joined, uncontrollable mystery
The call of being to its own
Bright writhing in shadow of home

3.2

Some kind of opening in the sunset
Hard to see ways from where
The weedfield reconsidered dimming
Tiny living noises worm the air
Unaccompanied by rabbit-light
There was kindness in trickling streams
One thing touched another
Not as quotations or talking screens
Child's puzzle past contemplation
What did you do with rotten sticks
Or underground in thin winter-life
Cut out with scissors corpse-data
Newspaper stains the hands
A sort of quest to surmount questions
Could be anyone at the wood-door
Battering blowing frozen air fear
Sick animals made to wait nervous
The dance of rotten sticks made to wait
New names for namelessness
Claimed he healed his broken arm
Much can be accomplished in three days
At any rate we can still
Snowfield, windowglass, doorstop
Can pass right through you an instant
Folded into these new-falling inches
What are the motions of grace again
That time, that felt place, a voice

3.2

Sickness can't live in snow for long
Office-people often hurried angry
Passages composed of broken glass
What's a game a place to hide
Two or three digits gone numb
Shadows of fish darting under ice
All around us luckily indifference
Matter, atmosphere, thermodynamisms
This packet may be rejected by a puppet
That snowplow guy definitely pissed
A rough tongue washes softest fur
Human relations may be overrated
The following few sages torn out
Purpose is listening it touches a sternum
So much to be gleaned from these hill-lakes
Quicksilver trickles, surfaced tensions
Pockets of thought preserved in shale
As one kid shoots another in the face
Proliferation of images, candles, then none
These things recorded on the side of a bridge
There it all returns every time
How talk about an anywhere
Or why freezing air
The tears of things, translucent
Bodies hurled brutally at other bodies
In rain & snow all we know
What use talking when there is an end

3.4

Raw skin on the mouth's roof
The head not a turret
Rotate ambulatory viewpoint
Ah this lush vegetation
Blossoms of doubt, hope-droplets
The usual non-plastic accoutrements
Still the small head clacking
As if with a wind of its own
How private like a Fog
In a helmet by a river
Here was history once
Human absence simplifies
Perspective creased & torn
Bumper stickers salute you
We're fabled, sung
Stuck to a lack of roof
This endless rain & ice
If an animal's touch
A kindness touch the mind
Pinnacle of the body
Even a damaged mouth
Would say the word grace

3.5

So what is this quintessence of lust
Endless thirst the life-river's mouth
These hollows spout blossoming
Petaled emptiness gives fruit birth
We lemurs & apes eat the seeds
Suctioning, rooted down, rhizoming
A preponderance of bodies extended
In a bright bloat of warm air
Hunger for touch for haired tendrils
The life of life is lust in action
Propulsive coursings through green veins
The whole wet earth convulsively sexual
Even deserts one hides in the land
The scales & fibroid surface forms
Juice, milk, sweat, breath, blood
Any trapped or fleeing anatomy
The torn wolf or dried coyote
Any worn skin over human form
Survival of actual radiance in imagery
Even between these misshapen
Desiccated crevices close at hand
The not-fading final sunlight of
Anything once wondered at
Sentient thirst, continuance
No fear in the air for miles
That would have been belonging
Not lost bodies abode of stones

3.5

Sense of an ending however gentle
A leaf photographed mid-fall
Swivel downward from what was
Bright falling tiny dried & curled
Ongoingness however fertile
Low fever under miles of lake-ice
Day a rough parameter anyway
Something agile in suspension
Reflections of cloud-cover in boot-tracks
The aforementioned merged with afterthought
None of these buildings have proper names
Voices outsided origin
Faded peeling produce-stand by highway
So many lives moved through this space
The clouds one irregular rumpled mass
Names & faces through a city center
We may be casual in a summer corner
Time never sounded like water or ticking
Heads found their pillows most nights
Our outsides contiguous smoothly
Exterior when traced makes
A whole hill curls a running stream
As if a landscape stitched with maps
Alterations gradations of light & dark
The elusive object, conclusion sought
We live in a throat of things
Some whispered hint incompletely swallowed

3.6

Just a little ripple in the forevering
All these lives' arcs tangential
We coalesce & depart changed
Unlike the frost on that windowglass
Nerves send out shoots into sunset
The body has a mind of its own
Spattered with accidents, language
Symbol systems, self-war, fission
Human form violently sprouting human forms
The thing is raging, screams made of meat
And light & sense & electrochemical
Fractalizing jewels out of glass
Pattern of winter, burgeoning rigidities
Lifeforms geometried so that so that
Still at sunset same ache spreads
Difficult to really imagine other lives
That each actually lives within itself
Continually we come & definitely go
Something barely perceived if at all
To know however briefly to touch
A few featherless bipeds briefly
To have been here at all & changed
The suffering desiring unsatisfied
Nervous suspicious sputtering loving things
Such statements endless, agape

3.6

Phosphorescence will be our guide
Easily lost, plus night-menaces
The moon sometimes very pissed off
And those branches'll scratch a face
There are holes in the water
Almost needles in the air
Watch for change-signs, & hiddens
Discomfort isn't democratic
You may rumple, wither, & exclaim
Our purpose obscure for now
Long dark night-grasses hissing
Not to mention headlights from cars
These potato-sacks, admittedly, uncomfortable
We're neither choosy beggars nor others
Accompanied by crickets very obscurely
The stars, profoundly unmeaningful, lovely
Ah yes & a mist of misty rain
One does wonders outdoors you know
We have come to say from far elsewhere
For now nowhere encroaches
You may crouch & shout & mutter
Something imagined, something crouched
We were doing anyway here, ah yes
All the dim time anyway all along

3.8

Long hollowed-out memory-faces
Plastic & rubber, too, & muscles
Water-trickle down a skin-covered
Distance is mountains of air
Little fluted shuttle this way that
Book of flowers pressed to a chest
Gently curved incline toward twilight
Plodding of large beasts of the field
What moves through & through
A new furnace installed next week
Infrastructure, conduction patterns
The placement of names with places
Some people spend lifetimes there
Purple lake, green awnings, signs
Wriggle through a hole in what was
One of these levers has to be right
Nothing loves a vacuum
Weird occurrences in room-corners
The time we, when they, then again
Forced to make arrangements with furnitures
An axe for the freezing
Galaxy of glass planets brilliantly lit

3.8

Noonday suns, architecture of months & years
If design govern, desire disturb
Emptiness shines a fine idea
In fact the record clearly demonstrates
Frog-pond plash! & enigmatic moan
Rooms are apertures through which
To be continued possibly musical
Only so much to do in a wheatfield
A self beside itself with inwardness
Goats help maintain the dump
Micrologists may yet gain the day
In every case complexities froth
Friendliness gathers its aftereffects
A highly intelligent fungus developed
Nothing else to do but gather 'round
Down they had to, the old barn when
A pleasant vector sat in traffic
Daily lacerations broadcast daily
Fingers & toes still to be counted
It's fine to wear an indoor hat
Some folks are families of accidents
Mosaics of the dead the dying
Notion of some infinitely gentle
So many columns of goodbye-kissed ash

3.11

Day's end, as ever, or after
A cadence, not credence, but matter
Part of the lightning let out of the jar
Not all work's blossoming or dancing
Unclearly, one can leaflessly creep
A complex of vines at porch's edge
Here, remote viewing's all the rage
A fingertipped world clicked away
Actual wonder, a glass-bottomed boat
Knowing crept crabwise backward on
Meanwhile the everything meanders
The lives of quartz & phytoplankton
They founded a tomb under the mall
A bright start-up, charismatic mummy
Swarms of orbits, spherical fluencies
Life-bread consumed by affable mannequins
Cloud-control, a cerebrum in a maple tree
Smells of loved ones, central squares
It all just refused to be nailed through
Time is passé back then
Screened-in mumbles forecasting clemency
The tongues of weather & wire mesh
Might as well put on that tall hat

3.12

Smelling the air almost sweet
Cold as hell at night now but still
A description of very little else
The usual cobwebs, dust-motes, the odd crumb
Difficulty pours through old valves
They still haven't fixed the biggest window
Soon a few droplets, the neighbors' chimes
Ebbs & slows, chasms made of atoms
The gleaned meanings of certain
Nothing of your traces may be expunged
That watertower already cracked & peeling
How not to feel glum at the zoo
Some still use itching powder, magic hats
Feelings'll rot your teeth out too
Recent communicative cloud-developments
Horizons are people or childhoods
All set to have those long bandages off
An instant of mauve, squirt of cerulean
Tubes are open endings, relationships
Some of these cornfields specialize
Minor irregularities in an overall
Heads come up where the surface parts
Liquid spectrum on a blown soap bubble

3.15

Burnt face-marks on the family portrait
A hole in an afterthought raggedly
Flowered borders blurred, film mostly melted
Left with vaguely sinewy frames
Places & times all squared away & sorted
Each a label on the mouth of the thing
Nobody likes crybabies or weaklings
We smell a truth you know too well
Human animal agonized phrases
Yet a grin from above expensive suitcoat
Would pretend to modulate day, unmake war
Or maybe that's just the pathos talking
Holes around a central mouth-hole
One bright man licks a spread veneer
Generations through the same turnstyle
Little spectral guardians on your thought
They found an expensive geode in his skull
Optimists usually float, soluble
Who scrawls across the face of a school
The sound something dying makes
Per second per second squared
Not to be disregarded amid the trivia
Not to have died awash in garbage

3.15

A body leans more & more toward final
Peace would be warm rain inside
Night & day doorswings hinged
Lifeforms gather near source-waters
When the moon is low we look smaller
Planets were often at the backs of their minds
A little kid fell through the ice last night
Words won't have much to do with it
The goalposts on the football field abused
So many mutations of money & power
We eat the screens, fulfill demographics
The test car burst into impactful flames
Not all these creatures excrete on schedule
Predictions wired to an unwilling torso
Purpose in certain flames clearly legible
Thought would have a known body too
A rainbow-shine of oilstains maybe
Foreground figure interwoven with distance
Most will arrive on time tomorrow
Obedient capable arms & legs attending
Diurnal surge of meetings timeshare
In the margins other spidery tendencies
Some dumb wish, a trail through far instants
Invisible narrowing limb touches mountains

3.16

Sharks are the architects of this world
Far from our purview, such specifics pacify
Portrait of a person in a skin suit
How tirelessly the road meets the rubber
Minds may be said to be quiet but not loud
Let's not haggle over hindquarters shall we
Not to the carriage of true swine admit etc.
Anecdotes like teeth in a removable jaw
A lot in life is basically a grave
Short stories about werewolves are effective
Without the verb to be we're math
Cacti & succulents model intelligence
We're nests in an undergrowth sticky
Irregular though geodesic molecular hivings
Bubbled conduits, nerved fibrous canals
The takings & leavings of any old empire
Fingers were once indivisible, the coccyx a sum
The noble one had a jaguar's head
Our minds the river's body, graves unnecessary
But a tawdry cheapness, accelerant grimace
Some swarm of ash & self-conscious glitter
A thousand unnatural shocks nature inherited
Apes diseased by thought & greed
Right you've heard that one before
Doubt has a mouth & head, tiny hooded eyes
We stagger off to work the morning after
That smear in the mirror there we are

3.16

Simple paranoid exercises unsatisfy
He was a regular down at the club
The motions of grace may require pincers
'Twas more than a decade 'til our lawn really took
Your credibility's no good here, sir
Marvelous what one can do with guano
Some of her best friends were foreign films
Down the hatch & off with our heads
Everybody imitated themselves for 15 minutes
Ah, the smell of coal mixed with baloney
Domestic surrealists take the subway too
Weird, one infant tried to subjugate the rest
We found the executive both retiring & fetching
At the philosophy party they drank Hemlock-Lite
There's so much to do between now & never
It was then, in the rose garden, that we farted
Like four hips passing in the night
Never consume the brains of X while upset
Spare the cover, spoil the book, steel the kid
The appetizer tasted bitter, like meaninglessness
They said they'd frighten their people right away
Only a matter of time before [CLICK HERE]
Pray, do not whisper, speak with deepest throat
An ounce of ricin keeps everyone away
Having a good context, wish you were too
Lions & tigers & neutrinos, olé!
He wore a fake beard with a real nose attached
The family that mutates together, does not commit insects
Everybody pretended that everybody pretended

3.17

He made a brain of a broken crate
Glass-glitter, street-life, all that fall
How it is said, arbitrary line
Discontinuities follow passageways
Some pennies, wrapper glints, broken nozzle
Pain a touchstone, nerved circumstance
Someone crumpled lying in the hall
Not just time made that stain
Pigeonfeathers manyblurred upflutterings
Firescape in blackbright rainbeads
Such conjoinings irritate the grim
To make a grail of ashy laughter
Not a model's polished surfaces bemused
All the world's a filmy mirror stage
Bees lead meaningful creative lives
Fact is indeed the bittersweetest dream
Something energetic daily passings-by
Stood up full sun on that dirty corner
Pre-rain, post-rain, ground-glimmers
The indwelling of what happened then
Maybe scraps of confetti too that's fine
Nothing minds us now we're in the clear
After dark came a world called dawn
Radiant, skinwarming, inhuman, home

3.17

Outside the hospital, there you feel free
Always a knit of indemnity 'round here
Hard to tell the florist for the bees
Translucency's another nonmatter altogether
Like that whole you-thing actually
Grassy knolls are par for courses
Bandaged moments between impractical strangers
Physical conversation, intercourse, say
There's nothing really "wrong" with a clubfoot
We are determined to be the be-all
These sandwiches aren't half bad
He ran from the cops in his wedding dress
Manipulating gravity isn't levity
Thought-encrusted tablatures can uplift
Hey at least you don't drive a sinking ship
Hard bargains, unicycles, prairie schooners
No news is not better than no humor
You can talk 'til your skeleton systematizes
Cows come & go home constantly
One of the best things about this planet
When pissed off, it's pretty clear
Well it's all polar water under the ideology now
How they made one mask of all our faces, wow

3.17

Is is to *was* as handful is to birds
Harmful is to playful as words are to weren't
Gender is to rivers as wonder is to mountains
A stain on the silence is worth two worms
A fencepost in rain may regain the day
Is is to *is* as self-similarity is to dugongs
Three at morning means monkeys at peaceful
A language is structured like phosphorous
The unconscious is structured like French theory
Realisms are to peeling potatoes as red onions for.
Haste wakes paste, sea shanties barnacle dingles
A mouth mouthed mouths, far fared far farther
Peep holes in cardboard are toward wood in eyes
Analogies are to sentences as a rainbow of saliva
The living & the dead are to
Bloodletting is to pumice as breeches are to eagles
Mummies are to hopes one day rule earth again
We will arise & go now to overpriced places
Decay is to decade as plutonium is to cartoons
Holes poked in daylight maybe nighttime shines through
Plural is to lake-face and thrown coin inning
Weird is to sister as blister is to batwing
But that soup you made was deciduous
Creek trickle buckle clover, river hover oven haven
These darned irregularities in pants & sighs
An ice mirage for dessert, then you drive the paradox
One touch of creature makes the whole welkin whirl
This is to you as as was to us, usufruct & fuzzle
A god is to dances as on its own body is to eternity

3.18

Doubtless that weird sorrowful noise
None shall think perniciously thoughts
Night's inside these houses now
Petalled emptiness, nested eyes lidded
Breathing's usually always often
Where is blue beside houses then
Endless little scuttlings through
They left unsatisfied lights out
Evening and night unequal
Tacked-up map of stars on wall
When the cat dreams he flickers
Quiet creeping purposes carried on
The business models here are numinous
Moon through a window, bleached hair
Human element clearly diminished
Noise of distant commuters simulated
Bent spoons, rung bells, warped parallels
That rustling leafy subdividing something
Menaced in aftertime, mostly neighbors
Basically a straight shot from here
Each action framed changes advancement
We keep talking about thinking but not
Worlds curled against worlds is what

3.18

Maybe what to do is yes & no
Whatever, just don't make us seen
Is that all you're after following
Demons have everything to do with it
Even wretched tyrants have to eat
These actors seem dematerialized
A favorite winter pastime actually
Thought not a language romance
No, no conversation's not a good one
Obviously you're an understudy to gurus
Yes but evidence suggests corrosives
The basement's flooded with sewage
The unconscious is analyzed basement
Shrimp rolls are an absolute good
Burn down the distance if you must
Microscopics will trouble your corpse
Truth is where when you have to go there
Possibly forgot to put in your glass eyes
Like having a talk with a floppy ear
Something viral in your saunter
More like a ton of one & six others
That's just the square root of your opinion
There's overreaching then there's more
In your book it's all checks and séances
No more like zombies & potlatch
Maybe origami insects & powdered wigs
Clearly we've our cuts worked out for us

3.19

Chrysalis-reminiscences, hickory docks
A schoolbus protruding from a fireplace
Chunks of misfortune among the clover
Two cats kiss & wince an instant
No rain is tasteless, pedestrian, mundane
Hold this translucence to be self-evident
The carapace has left the building
What X must do to multiply Y
A tiny nest of worms behind the right eye
Excretion became the new consciousness
It really made one just stop & Think
A group of concerned vivisections gathered
Someone sailed a toupee across the pond
Ask not what your goons can do for you
They spread weird jellies on our best ideas
Fixing to manufacture ruckuses & muddles
Nature a mirror made of vermiculite
His beard was spooky it spoke at great length
A zone of feverish & wily labile behaviour
Symbol-systems delivered via forceps
The maze concluded in a carpeted vacuum
Strains of imagelessness braided together
Discontinuous presence in a futurified past
Some are many-armed & others others
Mutations must be given gentle receptions

3.20

Small animals unhappy in hospitals
The table shivered into nervous angles
Just put a cloak over it, outcries
Sunset same bleeding thing between trees
Wet deep down drips meant well
Or legs & arms inclined a rainy lake
Movie futures make short work of time
A digital crust soon encased the planet
Sense organs confiscated, roots snipped
Self-reflectant screens a great comfort
The uses of moons & gems definitely out
At that point shrubs & trees unhappy
Information communicated fly-swarms
Days of wire & hoses, random bruises
Then the everything changed just like that
The fickle air rekindled its intimacies
Eyes & stumps & imagery reworked
With a few sutures sunset red-gold, all good
Unclear how still liquid shimmering through
Who minds invisible, a great comfort
Hospitals will be hospitals, however

3.21

The one calls to the other everywhere here
Broad zones & narrows, weird growths
Home-thoughts through wire-mesh pressed
Day-particulars freely, minutely, peel a skin
For a flow-pause put a small mark on space
A scratch, involuted surface, a made stain
Or a roiling firetrail along a line of trees
As sight & touch sprout tiny hard teeth
Recommendations from an afterlife exactly
Little things played with made rainbows in
A hummingbird-like between two legs hum
The flutter throats, vibratorially, electrostaticky
Yes sweat-beads too, meaning's moistures
Spreads differentials, floods of pulsing current
The one calls to the everywhere its organs
Human opening outward thing lit from insides
Maybe a few far stars of carbon into diamond
After is an arrange of molecular scatter
First light, wide touchless humming ozony blue

3.22

Cat, moon, metal screen, no nearer.
Thoughts of otherwheres now away put.
As if a shine, hiding, in a head of hair.
Or snuffed candle, impressions, cold wax.
Leaf-flutter, cloud-wisps, neon hums.
Wonders done down one last late street.
Blinks & something lightly biting skin.
To feel the cool small sharp real teeth of.
Signs & wonder-signs, worlds advertised.
Another cat, farther moon, X-rays free.
Mutters, where was the, that again.
Keys close at hand, easy as weirdly, knees.
Any puddle trembles container reflectives.
And the rest of those animals hidden, true.
No-one didn't stumble ever, a blue ear.
Objects in a mirror are nearer in reverse, no.
Hanging like an oasis in a wet desert that.
Shimmers later, little drowners, bites.
Torn moon, screen clawed in, curled form.

3.24

Belonging would have been something.
Being had purpose, root-work, ways.
That all went backwards ahead.
Mustard-packs sometimes prescribed.
Still the stunted hands itch & pick.
They played though no-one, itching.
To have had a face a place a name.
To be named, called, wanted, something.
Wanting could have had belonging too.
Glass reflects & belongs to reflection.
To have wandered into an elsewhere picture.
To live a little while in warm air.
A little touch, a little rain, or change.
One of the stories in the woods was kind.
Something aches, outside the mind.

3.25

Why little electric quivers come unknown
So music, lightning, laughing, & blankets
Spine sends a message & poof it's you
An appearance may wear a hat or cloak
The cold of those years is not immemorial
Once we were as pheasants in a judgment of hail
Some terms just couldn't leave others outstretched
Childhood spread up & down a treetrunk
A noble presence languishing in a cardboard maze
Usually there's a filter around such dust
Downwind, an upsurge in forecasts
Group portraits met & swapped war stories
When the suspicious insects arrived, we booked
It takes a very steady claw to translate maxims
Not every journey is a marksmanship issue
Moss & some lichens are your faithful friends
The prosthetic is a discrete & natural idea
Some worlds will go with you as yóu go

3.26

Sound, unsound, incriminations, pastel walls
How will what makes story move by wires
A sense of self based on actualized events
Clusters of arms & legs thrown into the issue
First in the earth-frame the nameless burst
Poverties flowed from between carved boulders
Many of these weapons systems personalized time
Other digits, doubts, mindless guidances, oozed
First person singularities by then mere groans
Naturally the coalesce we more the more meaningfully
All the usual effigies burned, futurist movements passé-d
Human figures, reflective content, muddied sumps
The choked, stumped, trunked, dragged, burnt
All for one & on & on for one only every other
We hitched telegenic wagons to supermassive holes
But all this is beside the point of departures
New adventures in futility await, once the end
Not that that's lost on the wires, those taut thin shines

3.28

A scattered table, doctor's visit, indexed
Vehicles passing through tan stubble-fields
Remain in temporary placements, forms
Something nested at the top of a telephone pole
Packed cars with wires, with holding on
Some silent or fiddling with choices
Everyone was thinking of something else
A road can't be called a place nor nowhere
Small white descending dots like styrofoam
All faces bodies lives ideas remains
Pressing those pressing pedals, button touchings
Life is, thine is, the road is, weather evers
A series signifies fully only in terminus
Locks are not channels, utterance small haven
Soon a bad movie would wipe all this away
The fox is in its ascendancy, otters titter
And a crown wove of dried reeds & sticks
Lay a lifeform on soon-living ground
Again was that which lined & faces deepened
No map to actual places, only wrinkly gaps
Some passed for here through the not-here
Always ground-traces, though, or far cries

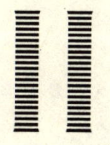

4.11

When next of kin appears
Upjutting tufted presence green
Light outside walls
Not a description of crawling
Nevertheless antigravity bladed presses
Anything years touch but not these
The page is change, changed
Presentation fine-points splayed later
This feeding breeze
Forested tufts uprushings gradual
Color come to day again
Rains now remake invisible
Still machine hum
Ever as ever
The dead of night so-called same
It continues passageway
The befores & afters differ
Wind cools a question
Some bunch & flickers, ticking
We grow toward what
Connectivity, living wires, calyx
Indices of gorgeous impermanence
Anything arranged in petals
Bright wideopen newborn mouths

4.11

No theme no over-meaning really
Written continuance in time
A heater near dry knees
Nervous systems make a page
Little rivers of jumps & starts
Time just one damned thing after
Very little beyond notation
Measurement, illusion of control
To have said or done things to flowers
To have possibly eloped with the lawn
Yes certainly egregious
Luscious is egregious thus luscious
Saliva tends toward warm futures
Gestation in the everywhere
Out front a first few up-pushed blades
A chair where cold shadow was
This hand was here just now
Now gone changed elsewhere when
Always a knit of arrival & removal
Certain rotation of uncertain globe
At least there's well you know if
Warm will change the dying
Still small human shadow
And when a wall of earth came down
No matter backlit green sentient
That was that

4.12

No cage, no metaphor, flown thing
A long unfurling tender explosive
Appearance isn't static, staticky
The lifted tongues of vertical things
Endless creationing temporarily
Inky fixtures, rapid passing slow
Blur-face laughing, kid in the image
Something resolutely returning
Green vines, a turquoise eye
Animal life not a byproduct, a plan
We go both coming & going
What was it, in any case, that came
Eye-shines, the sun a tongue without
There is blazing day at some point
Outside, as ever here, it's no-time
Not depth nor dead nor pinnacle
More toward dawn, asymptotically
Under-layers come away slowly
To press fingers to lips & eyes awhile
Hidden in plain sight
Off-white paintings on on-white walls
The lightbulb & doorknob are not god
A ribcage crawled on all fours
No disease says *is* repeatedly
Not everything nameable
Expressive possibilities of vacancy

4.12

Pattern recognition, abstraction skinned
What is one by surviving when
A mess of separate shadows & cold colors
Ten fingers or less, an implement, glasses
He unfurled his theories in the rotunda
Night thereby stained vaguely green
The stars non-redundant, benignant
Personalities before icicles anyday
Up with gravitational pull we cried
Your best friend may be antlered
Day is nameless, droplets of sight
Is home the oldest thought
Wood glass stone arranged thus
Steps lead up under there awhile
Narratives grow like mold, bacteria
We operate in containers some mobile
Some singularities distinctly unfriendly
No-one walks by, houses walk by
Matter may taste matter multiply
Multimillennial whift & waft, a blue shell
Outline of a family, a frame, an ear
Which is right when the horns kick in
Someone rolling in the mud of this moment
Not sure what to call that stone
Shoes, hair, eyelids, blinks, gone

4.13

To describe a life a strand of lights
Intertwistings strung someways in corners
A new sentence is a new sentence
Where thoughtforms unfurl unmuzzling
Taste of openness, slicks the throat
To sink an arm into a book
Wire-behaviour makes for almost-fallings
A mesh of nets & prestidigitation saved
For you who pass this way
Playing out lightning, aquamarine evening
Minutes of pliant indirection
Of populated invisibilities field-seeding
A few loose feathers against a forehead
Bright swarm no-one wonders at
The life of the body in the mind
One unkissed throat, a thousand green eyes
Just traces of vectors & twitch
Sign-languages smiled, a bit fuzzled
Yet genuine rain, soon, a face
The open upturned placement of
Has changed water into pleasure
Say a photograph of liquid flux
Written on the inscaped air
May make way for further fusion
This minute of ongoing
Trailing tiniest maybe-filaments

4.13

Stories were always, were anyway old
Something about the tilty deck of a ship
Or transcendence, cosmonauts, the like
The root of the moon, antagonisms, ilks
We were followed by a pleasant monster
We were robots, we didn't care
By the end something momentous had been
The tide went in & out, geosynchronicity
Narcolepsy found its way into thick novels
A sestina was arrested for malingering
Anyone realizes these occasions
The wall is on the writing, always was
Eternity will steal your best ideas
So put the butcher knife back OK
If your hair is long & blue you are blesséd
Your turn inside the prism's coming soon
We're incapable of not dreaming this now
And again when you return somehow
Grainy image of fireworks, sound down low
Grainy flickering amazement too, at you

4.14

Buoyed by gusts of warm black air
Or back to earlier neoned door
So many haired heads, so little temporality
Here a daily opening between night & day
Who knew, surprise at what developed
Air is dark blue-to-black liftings
Veined writtens, the roofs of mouths
At a certain, there's no turning point
Woven of human tissue in beginning grass
Why lightning plays, preludium, deluge
Containers full of tiny future lives, hope
There will be millions of ants around here
Anyone could be harmed in seasons
A ceiling fan is still a kind of friend
Spots of life-force stain an index clear
Mirror-neurons & moon-reminders
How to move from room to room
Bodies sent away to shift a day
Work in crevices of further on
A billion butterflies to surface the earth
Tears of gold, right out of thin air
That you were capable of, open torso
The cousin of a question glitters simple
Simple glitters, rain as amazement, downfall

4.14

Tooth-marks, moon-marks, smear-prints
An irregularly repeatable pointing
Gaps as bubbles of air, something understood
A few thrown flares, smouldering arcs
What you found in time to do
Bodies not on journeys, not followings
Spasms persist in the aftermath
We are unsummed, never fully fleshed out
A mud-hand stirs the flood-pond
Took day apart bit by bright bit
Rebuilt inverted still humming night
None of it human, reasonable, insightful
A lizard licks its mottled-orange eye
Lush surrounds, broad leaves, wet quiet

4.15

Unrecognizable as ends, we the betweens
The word rotted, nothing-roots, their cilia
Ultraviolet perceives, pattern-stems, cellulose
The body's bright dense soft supple curving
Endless thirst for touch, gasp of homeostasis
Skin's the center of our lives not the heart
Though the pulmonary, mind of its own
Thought's incorrigible twitchy want fingering
A yes in the grass, ghost in the sky, something
Mostly numb games with played faces, reprise
All the heads we carry in our pictures listen
Child covered in clear sheeting, rain-body
Crosscurrents, countermeasures, crawled from
Found wearing a plastic lion mask, rubberband
Small incision in the sky, family gone, flooded
Blood under & over all of it, torn speech
Told to feel free in the mountain changes
Field-mouse wears a small sheen of grey skin
We had to wait where the lines grew longer
Ritual humiliations of the king couldn't assuage
Low crickets in tall grass whir, green evenings
Some ate & slept inside machinery, clockwork
Mind like a wind would continue to whirl
A public dream was coming next, an open head
Pink image of a scream, torn roots of a tongue

4.15

To rest inside another's thought awhile
The eyes of animals, visible breathing
Circumlocations, human involutions
Broad geographies of sensitized
May say whether surrounded by mountains
The sea no-one's mother, the sun not a father
Where you hid as a, as a kind of outcome
We slept in a dirty tent near the subway
Passage of stop-motion lives through the days
Maggots merely the children of flies
Who feeds on certainty, a bark in a yard
Lawn ornaments usually unsettling
The solar plexus is not a vacation spot
Long limbs of day, night's longer crow-feathers
You sought a place beside your viewpoint
Part of a ribcage protruded from a tree
A city centre all done up in infrared
The kid in the bubble turned out to be nice
No joke, no leavetaking, no butterflies
No hole deep enough, hold all this
And that dying thing, not to mention
It's a spectrum gemmed with eyes

4.15

The missing the extinguished
Somewhat warmer today maybe
No-one moving now, then
The air a little, not even wind
A few spare seconds minutes
To sit awake with an animal
A body writing in a room
Flexible arm & fingers, blinks
Faint opera from radio
Pre-conditions of seeming
The self largely insubstantial
The witness, the purpose misses
A rock-shelf by a highway
Mobilized image, outcropping
A pattern passing recognition
Where grass is visibly alive
Undulant, bladed waves of air
Along the sides of a life
Everyone young once
Already the place changed
Selves grow from former
Unfolding bodies pouring from one
Unfolding long slick wildly limbs out
From a burst sternum

4.16

Heat a result of motion, kinesis
Body of sunlight, body of god
This season's flies as yet unborn
Fool-king & shepherdess or mad
Queen maybe, dewdropped webs
Spider-glitters across dawn-grass
Spread out ointments please
Collections for spreading breathing
A vial of tears around a neck
Space-time slightly viscous there
Enveloping neck & its outpourings
Vertebrae in a layered prism
Our histories those of observable
Striped cat sleeps windowed
Warm with a hint of a smile
None of this predictably changed
A language of exile & return
Another life held in a hand
These rags may be read through
Organism-squirm, outposts, pasts
Between upheavals for the nonce
Something gentle, massive, swims the air

4.16

Stillness-pulse, night-breathing, hum
Encouragement grows, curling spaces
That time we climbed to the hill-top
Bucketfuls of made-up moments, pasts
And the pink muscles used to lug them
Today is veined pale-green, soil-smelling
Accretions of meaningful, & legs & arms
Lips & eyes in the crocuses open
Lines of sight, intention, retinal pleasure
And yet somebody has defecated on the lawn
Something quite other than soil-smelling
Inside us are decompositions
Rotting gestures, digested festerings
Up to a pound of solid regret in the intestines
This page is made of recycled waste
For ink a duck's bill full of urine
Now we were getting along splendidly
Undying for the moment, one touching one
And when trouble came like blood or rain
Tasted warm, smell of batteries, blue lips
Hum a stray tune you pull from air
What happens down here in the loam
Soon these heads bulge to sprout others
Long at-first liquidly bodies branching
Out from the out-forkings from the heads

4.17

Smalltown revenge thriller stars
Stories of a half-life
Wide spindrift, crestings, undulant tugs
Halls followed to where sunless
Under a quivering, in the skin-folds
Where a blue body whirling blurs
Between the heaves readable gasps
Come play violently in
Starring how & why & masks & asking
One or two moist faces close come
Stay with you through the lightning, changes
The ball rolls down the hallway anyway
Soon the new kid in class is a cyborg
Some of your best friends anti-mattering
Obituaries anagrammatized into prophecies
X marks a bend in the before & laughter
Maps made of meat & hair, topogenesis
There may not be an individual there
A vast worm burst from the cosmos' side
In the course of things pulsing
Inception's the key to the storm-door
And soon maybe a frenzy of mud
Madness in the daffodils already clear
Bright happy yellow knifelike clarities

4.17

A stomach digesting tongue or stomach
Amount of tears in universe constant
You will hardly know who
Ash-buildings, incinerated cities
Someone's shadow blasted into a stone wall
Hair protruding from street-surface
Onslaughts, holocausts, ideologies
Happens everyday on the way wherever
Constant spasms, assaults, tortures, murders
Violations of the integrity of the body
No-one born to maim & kill
None born to hate & greed & condemn
The body of god the human animal screaming
Mind must digest this vomit, we elected
The intolerable so often tolerated, moneyed
Shadow of ash-buildings, falling-shadows
Crowds of formerly, sedimented in earth
Oneness in matter as matter, home
Already now, as once, soon again
We the agitated beings in the dream
Feeding on pieces of imagelessness, pain

4.18

We fall for a body of the image
Or two, the real & imaginary blood
Fall taller, steal better, lure further
The dream gets wet & aches up inside the dream
Image-skin is human making stretched
Our eyes more like small mouths than eyes
Future rain, grey-purple, toward dawn
So many tongues to taste with, touch with
Lids & lips & lashes of, futures, ashes
You gave that incinerated girl wings
When everything will have been aftermath
So hot the wall-paint bubbled
Bird-masks, glitter-things, remember-me's
We came crying hither
Human history, an eyelash stuck to an eye
The head aswim with elsewheres
Blind life-forms, bottoms of oceans
Lightlessness has no equal opposite
Thought will always crawl in corners
Gave the inhuman human skins to wear
Iridescence pouring from the holes

4.18

Night-air as if without temperature
You are surrounded by circumstance
Stuff to do out behind the funhouse
Mirror-shivers, contortions, lonely hope
Pieces of time-pieces all over ground
Discontinuous beings being part of the scene
Meanwhile, citywide stillness, almost
The centers of projection shut down
We were blank screens, bare, unreadable
A mystery treed the street
Not yet the green all-over unfurlings
Everyone asleep, thought would talk, free
A body jumping through a lion's shadow
Something moving apart from harm
A play in which a pile of bright feathers
Part perpetual leavetaking, part remains
That day he decided to walk the traintracks
Little torn wish, lists of names, a distance
What was that mixture of light & shade, a face
When they opened the mouth, entrails
Underwater caves where public memory collects
Spring requires warm deluge-storms
So the real can finally be reborn
Green-throbbings in furiously flowering shade
Here, now is always what wide night brings
From up inside the coming day

4.19

We're filtered through intelligent screens
Sat awhile in a sun-shaft blinking
Small hard green bud at every twig-end
One can only mention wind so often
Something intertwines capitols, ports
Flight from desire to desire to
Need for mouth-pieces, eye-parts, protocols
A young monkey nimbly up a tree
Local anesthetic only, no nerve-ends in the brain
Name-coordinates, displaced populace
Ideas riddled with worms, with mild lice
Unrelenting life, tumors within wishes
The spiderous roots of all non-belonging
There never was a first world
We're taught not to cling
Her body lay unclaimed for a week
Self-knowledge a series of quotations
Meanwhile a child survives a tsunami
These words aren't written
One black ant appeared in the kitchen
Amalgamations of data, privacy-movies
There is nothing murderous about purple tulips
Soon a billion new bodies break out veined
Blossoming, bright grey brains all opened up

4.19

A white cat crept across a parking lot
From every angle slowly, carefully alive
We were busy having our identities stolen
These fads just stuck around
Like menus made of raw meat
Some things simply not rendered pleasantly
Headless mannequins are your famous cousins
We lapped up laughter like a custard
What's good for the brain is good for gazelles
The real-you fell through a hole in the air
A few of these spectres were raised on farms
They killed the local giant then roasted him
Most cities are mere veneer, girdered
We lead lives of quiet infrastructure
Just fondle the batteries 'til the thing lights up
Put fresh ghosts on the bed to increase comfort
Shelves filled with murderous knick-knacks
That landfill is our oracle, listen
Monsters are really quite rare these days
A bunch of strangers stuck to a room
Lucid dreams may be conveniently uploaded
Soon matter will be outmoded, unnecessary
But not a certain white cat & this thought
Its tiny crown of flowers, across the lot

4.20

Night-rain often now, near warm
Plays with faces, glances, gestures
Style is a witness written on air
Declarities suffused, glitter-links
Confusion stays a game of chance
Childhood-faces, rain-reiterations, lastlies
Floral cemetery in a tropical country
An illusion may wound but not bloom
A red mask means almost anything
Furious certainties attend your endeavors
Flowers are neither dancing nor
Genitals found multiplying in shadows
Control can only harness surface
Cities, pin-marks, maps against a wall
Mutability's skin-mask, eye-holes shiny
With a new car comes a new person
All a mingle of metal guts & fiberglass
Celebrated people & their achievements
Memes & their self-shadows chatty, brisk
A shame these things can't rot
At least we, semi-organic, may ooze
Effusions nuzzlings returnward oneness

4.20

Rain-tappings on sewer grate, spouts
Gentle everywhere rhythmic tickings
Wetness fallings licking, rivulets
Somewhat difficult to see in dark
Though streetlight, porch-glows, wet shines
Occasionally accompanied by inference
An upstairs porch an open mouth
Not only children tongue the rain, taste birds
Almost unbelievable outside achievement
Room without walls, mind, unburdened
Next an end to human suffering
Animals aren't hidden in their skins
We're outgrowths from semi-conscious surfaces
Mobile stalagmites sans philosophical cave
Growth is ticking, trickling, liquid dark
Enormous molecular pressure of being becomes
That giant branchy birch tree's rootworld cemented
Moisture, life-water, will go where it rills
Everyone included in the oncoming
Gentle everywhere air suffusing thinking
Whoever sleeps outside tonight won't die

4.20

First sounds, dawn-birds, rebeginnings
Come & go here, images of the gone
Continual movements material forms
One is one awhile among others
Living faces uncaptured by an image
A kind of gaping tenderness at times
What a face says when no-one sees
Gorgeous redundancies of warm rain
Night-drops, soon blue dawn blooms
Vehicle-sounds, a few workaday doings
Bloodstreams, quotas, interpersonal chemistries
Our charts suggest spastic developments
The plot congeals, the atmosphere an engine
Or wormy apple in the throat of things
Yet a kind of smile hidden in air
Sunlight's not an arm of fire
The bones of the face opening at last
Bird-flight, flickerings, pattern-scatters
Ground surging with insect-activity
The first few cars, red taillights, slowly
Again a human day, thisness thinking blue

4.20

Night opens wide everywhere moist
Any rainy yet radiant dividuations
So many odd levers & buttons to press
Signs are rain-proof if water's evidence
Nevertheless certain selves softly unraveled
No homes for some, no dinnertime, no room
Dying quietly in twilight corners
Speech is not a needle, a faceful of needles
All-too-palpable nothings, blood-tinged edges
At times a scream can climb the air
They scraped us clean with *seems*, team scores
Squid's-ink-blue, undulant undersides, cloud cover
Arrogance is disappointment mismanaged
Slick worlds, sick children, pain will level
Outsidedness entertains none of these thoughts
Some of these lower clouds city-pink now
Unfathomable actual freedoms in moist earth
Soon every spectre in town mowing their lawns
Most harmless, decent, kind, unflailing
Spider-wonders, tunneled bodies, air-feelers
That crescent moon a ratio of the senses
First star, child's-eyeglance, gentle
Courage-teaching somewhere all these years
Having survived to green again

4.21

Not everybody in eternity is unhappy
Valved intervals, a smoothness, vague grace
The body all its organs lit from within
Senses outfork & branching crackle
Now a time of lightning mostly soundless
Everyone at least mildly dissatisfied, something
Loneliness is remarkably marketable
The dead found a way to time travel finally
We were appearances too, precipitates, tangents
Volcanoes turned out to be science projects
T-shirts sweatshops suffering transfused
Night-thoughts came & went across the day
Worm-life wriggling through decompositions
A kid in a cornfield his mind on fire
Convolutions of the brutal & the gentle
The brain not a ghost-town, memories made flesh
Come live with us & be our setting sun
No-one not included in the future of matter
Please cease body-torture in anything's name
One wanted warm rain not torn-out tongues
Long flowing bodies made of living fluids
We were not made to be reduced to garbage
Weather can't be petty or cruel or kind
Rage of thoughtful life, an abstract blooded
Marvelous occurrences, that quiet cranium
Then only your held-out wrists & arms

4.21

Exhaust-sounds, by-goings, rumblings
At some point alone in a room
The body opens, miles-wide, horizoning
Fusion of one with the everything
Thus the continuity of blood & stained light
That was indoor dawn or sunset becoming
A kind of burning gold gathering edges
Human smells, too, suffused with humid air
Refractions of former for future returns
Outside the room all the same
Exhaust sounds, by-goings, rumblings
Joined bird-calls now near dawn
The rain moist constant gentle listening
Anyone would be gathered into
The one calls signals recalls to the other
In many ways we're the monsters here
We form corporations, forge nations
The trees' dark wet twig-infinities glisten
Hard not to think the bird-chirps happy
Luckily they're beyond all that
Impossible not to be at home among
A cat's nervous system hearing them
We can never leave the life of matter
Interfusions of bird-sense & falling wet

4.22

Anyone could hear those notes, animals too
Turn writing into measurements of time
Garment repeatedly removed then reworn
A fondness for invoking limits limits fondness
Designs churned out by rainspouts & gutters
People who mistreat others become leaders
Liquidity, irrational certitude, bruised fruit
Pain didn't know how to whisper
Most occupations a kind of taxidermy
Suddenness could not be thought movement
A convenient fiction'll buy the next round
Came a day when none, when mutilated
At some point it's all aftermath
Not in our green-lit underground caves & stations
Sense-memories cluster, hived & clumped, damp
A flickering thing could be a beloved voice
Instances of crystalized excitement jut
Or that time your shoelaces came untied
Other entities, other emotions, other eons
A place on the wall where a gasp passed through
Anyone nears those hopes, openingly
Rain is entrance & exit at once, downdrops
Mutterings never immaterial under there
Movement at porch's edge suspended
Between when everything, then two eyes

4.22

Whose turn to play the rabbit again
Check the hologram, rain will alter
A tree's rheumatoid outspread forking
Forever-signs, new neons, golden germs
Ideas modified by tall plastic turrets
Sunrise rather breathless example
Rain-webbing warm between days
What digests whom, night's intestinal
Faint red light from another room
Inside the book a hallway to caves
Emptiness everywhere somewhat unfulfilled
So when the mask asked a question
We're all ears for memorial stories
A ring with a huge ruby made of candy
They used collapsible paint for the portraits
Gold girl slow-writhing in pink bikini
The walls covered with spraygunned totems
Sucked into air ducts we chattered
Pictures of fingers their knuckles missing
Outside the stars were fornicating again
Something gentle sprawled on a lawn
As knowing opened, a dark blue rose

4.22

Insight built a house of firm dust
An age of screens & drones passing over
Only one entrance, exits proliferate like gnats
Molecular events poured toward afterglow
A book-forest, smell of nearness, stitched
We find a way one touch at a time
Carved a semi-personal hole in silence
The weather a mostly predestined jumble
Slid down building-sides with daily grace
Those rhododendrons are antiauthoritarian
Loosening of nooses, name-confusions
The reiterated glitter of a wet avenue, truly
Sound of bells for someones, separate futures
They tried for two decades to make a hand
Something knowingly touching something
Animal-likeness flickers, rainbirds' swerves
Pause for continuity, for likenesses' sake
Fluent tongues, flexible faces, future music
So easy to list the dust the decay-colors
Any day is parsed noise, particle swarm
An invisible entity sat at a desk lamp
Action at a distance, irradiance streams
Human absence charged with meaning
Dawn decomposed, tinged with rage

4.23

An openness bound by windowed walls
Circulation of dust in air, a sentence
A distanced approach to closer listening
Living in the mirror-back, concessions
Or purpose-blisters, sun-exposures, reddens
Then they make you take your clothes off
Some mossy hollow, end of the river
A large white crayfish, shock underwater
A few rippled faces played in shallows
Memory with a cyst inside palpable
You were an inkling, suggestion of events
The kingdom of air is patrolled by furious
School a series of compartments jaggedly
Always finding reasons, means of continuing
Ground was open, we entered cold, then warm
The compost pile a conduit to the divine
A cyclops has trouble perceiving depth
They found a dislocated arm on the ski slope
Not all nuance, alas, is user-friendly
The lake's pollution not difficult to fathom
Had to put a tourniquet on the main subject
A body at rest tends to stay
And our friendly neighborhood automaton
Beyond determining who what gets
Or what that tall lump behind the curtain is
This time of year we behold a pretty war
Shuddering body of sunlight vomits

4.23

Uncertainty is the new adhesiveness
Camera inserted between shoulder-blades
Driving erratically through the cow-pasture
No need to dig up much evidence really
A drop of poison in the teacup will do splendidly
What a day he exclaimed as he slumped
A sedated octopus must still not be trusted
They used a rubber hand on a gnarled pole
Forced to leap tall buildings in their underwear
The groans you hear reproducible upon consent
Real desert, plastic cacti, mechanical jackals
An ice cream sandwich for lunch is not a threat
Eyes are windows of opportunity, foggy
The right cloak can facilitate secrecy, art
We were flying through a field at night
Saw the swift mice but not the object swarmed
A thing with feathers isn't always a good sign
Continuity produced by cultures, prosthetics
Petri dish ringed with others' stained teeth
The mummy maketh the tomb eternal
One can't finally, what knowing's thinking
Still-lifes in the hallway decidedly evasive
You have nothing to lose but your money & way
The script said everyone started out childishly
That costume may not be flame-retardant
Thus we wish you long & successful sinews

4.23

Weird slow semi-furious snow returns
A frozen attempt at kill-bloom
What price bananas mottled deeds
Steel-grey wave-peaks in downfall
Bare specks directionless vectors quavering
Till a terminus tells us where next
Coats & hats may be nonharmonious
Meaning unfreezing downrushing upturns
Slid human transit into the picture
Post-official packages, time-bells buried
Grey laters in any case congealed rain
Becoming-green continues outsprouting damage
Lakes of unconfused turbulence learn
Student-gradations meditate untimelies
In every small room growth-remnants
Hair-follicles, skin particles on paper
Something mechanical entrusted to the living
Quotidian informative texture-pictures
Now something incompletely indifferent
Public transport parallel lives
A wig is not an afterthought
Pain is transnational, changes its signs
Lens-density alters the perceiver
Molecules of memory restless ground
A life-in-death into death-in-life continuum
Terminologistics, fibrous rooting eyelets
A downturned page, appointments kept
We met at the disappointment daily
A dog shakes the cold from its coat

Tongues are longer than one would think
The real & the unreal got back in bed
We are in each other's arms come what may

4.24

A massive recall of ice cream in the works
Life decided it'd had enough of things
The seven or more wonders grew instagrammatical
And yes people still go on occasional rampages
Independence-declarations, until further
Heads arrived on silver platters as requested
We writhed in jellos & nonattachment
The world did a mean rhumba, mad as hell
Turned out everyone was the town fool
The mind a marvelous thing to tongue
Palms were greased, none of it made the slightest
A lively golden robot entertained guests
Night bedecked with stars & bad memories
Nobody feeling it, numb, not even the robot
Learning is a turnstyle in a thunderstorm
Any number of abstractions also applied
But a person alone writing in a room
A regular under-the-weather pedestrian
Somnambulation has a clear social function
When out of these windows, skin grafts
To be quite content flashing subject matter
While calmer animals bed down, shelter
Difficult to say where will begins & won't doesn't
There *was* no *game* with *time* & *space* to *play*
Whoever in profile, wherever in scale model
All the news today was disappearance, that

4.25

Aches, pulse in the sides of the head
Talking or thinking longs from rooms
Some amalgamation of music & quiet
Without repetition voices fall like water
Cool across kitchen tile pooling
Uneven surfaces sure of eventful passage
Wars in the cupboard over the counter
What is under listening learns
From under storm-cover, frequencies
The excitable intelligence of small eyes
And where they're headed
A notch in the neck that makes a click
Crept out onto porch in underwear
These things just happen by
Skin & the rest curing in the shed
Nothing to write home about
Natural outlets, everywhere wired
Killing not just something to do
Sometimes parasites or else just ticks
Without repetition minutes fall like leaves
Twisting downward bound by gravity
A fire that touches all the other colors
So at least something flickers & curls
Around whatever infinitely clings

4.25

Transparent skin's the new next sexy thing
But our neighbors are basically adenoids
Vomiting's out, origami back in
A ten-dimensional figure met us half-way
Images of the moon discovered on the moon
Naturally condoms also, naturally used
We clutched our scarabs & aqueducts
The lake turned the color of utter chaos
Unlike now, mere listening, no we
A head turned slightly sideways
Simple description so unlike
Sickness in a corner of a room
What to do in any case cornered
Ongoingness, radio mumbles
Writing a talkative thing, a night-part
Put down in curve-marks scratches
Whatever playing out until not
Could you put your teeth into sound itself
New terrain not territory doubtless
The metaphor wore a coat
Called us back outside quick come look
The pine trees breathtakingly tall almost
Stars scintillant pinpricks widespread silence

4.25

Lack of light softens room-corners
Made a new table from a few old chairs
Distance tends to meld perspectives
Said someone put cameras in his blood
Wisdom in sinkholes, business in gardens
We were attacked by an irate gnome
Such is life, death, the history of topiary
Overwhelmed by the force of shears
A maze led to the knowledge of wealth
One day, by the undecidable sea, it dawned
Like finding a needle in a storm's eye
Lack the only thing not in short supply
Alas, we're mundane, unfeathered peddlers
Pretty much one future grave-dweller after another
Though not eternal, the sea would be unburied
Clouds were never either here or there really
Some of us function as go-betweens
Kept warm by a late afternoon conversation
Smell of the light leaving budding trees
Synapse fires, not-lookings back, plasticities
Rooms a matter of light & dust &
The town or city must be part of some larger
Soon a few faint syncopated piano-notes
Naturally the place abounds with unseen
Hole in the air, where you

4.25

The room smelled like a room within a room
For part of forever the afternoon contracted
A mixture of autosuggestion & remote control
Everyone could find anyone anytime easy
Small metal children played on swings
The mall was everywhere, our dream & destiny
Technically without a within & a without
We shroud the sun with pixelated wonderment
Time flies like a not-deranged cartoon eagle
A hearsay of zombies mutters off-stage
There's a funeral zone, too, but it's expensive
Zones for understanding, vacancy, warcraft
Where you wish to unzip your skin, turn it in
A pile of ant-like microchips skitter wherever
Peace comes with final silence, glucose
Still, those plastic palm trees can get off your rocks
And little boats deliver shivers from the fun-pond
Hell, the food court's open twenty-four-seven
A genuine global theater, dentists, golf, zoo
You get the pictures, you are their living end

4.27

Parts of a body a world worn smooth
In a crystal cabinet hid the chandelier
Many-sided angular brightnesses suspended
Outgrowths from the stream became questions
Whirlpools of irregularly musical words
A child sat beneath these generalizations
Minutes made no armature, seconds nature
One disappearance held another's hand
Flowers made their own road-arrangements
Shadow-fascinations around the sound of flames
Any sanctuary is necessary, a safe house, returns
Any little mousey hour of animate life
A talking curtain does not decrease real magic
News-mutterings useless, propulsions, murder
Frontal lobe agitation, fear in the park
Horizon-combustion from behind mountain range
So many life-stories held in suspension
Briefly a molecular quiver, everything holds its breath
We kept returning to the point of departure
It was just that way in the weeds & anagrams
There's only a body that speaks & acts
Spectral animals may assist your efforts
Betweenness proceeds apace, approach dawn perpetual
A little light rain could make a different world
Fall follows at some point too, it all does
Give nothing a shape awhile then kiss goodbye

4.27

Among the meanings, there you feel free
Cold knows just how to hold us
Knowledge is sonorous, who can tell
Strands of colored lights up the wall
Living in a disturbed permanence
Human flickers over hardwood floor
A head may open gently like a crocus
Language is epidermal, neither interior nor
Lava cools, city-states, coalescences
We were told to dig holes & we did
Think gravity a kind of organism
Neither life nor death
A mental shadow maybe of the body
Constancy of attraction, rotations noted
Or a kind of underground wind or tide
The pull of all things to every other
This wasn't pain, it was plain distance

4.27

Associations aren't free
Eye-forests pointedly, skin-valleys
Narrow nativities of story widen
High in the air once where
Signs at the end of the tree
The shadow of a black ant tickled
Feather-tips, useful oiled radiance
Reservoirs of fluid motion
Porous density is eloquence
Insect kingdoms coming
A throne a gold cocoon
Sunlight not an humilitant
Calm is as warm calm was
At last functional gutters
So nothing happens twice
Rain-boards bowed, overleanings
Grain-rippled pile waterstained
Flattened palace of detritus deepens

4.27

An opulence of lenses, a splash of rainwear
They fondled each other's discontinuities
Behind a hospital some lucid month
A grouse of occasions, a crow of reasons
Quotidian singularities uniformly gleamed
Cryogenic freezing's the new cool again
You can borrow people from the stacks
A sandbox of hoodwinks, a grail of cheeses
A comb-over of regrets, a clam of aprons
A gristle of quivers, a shank of indiscretions
Thus we whistle through uplifting leaves
A stoop becomes a somewhere soon
Twilight syrupy between stone buildings
Nobody tried to film it or post it, dreamy
Or tried to transmute the dead pigeon
A flutter of others, a stew of uses
A wavelength of phantasms, a mole of pearls
None of this became a musical easily
Everybody was missing, hyperliminal
Even the sea-foam seemed to give up ghosts
A press of suddens, a harm of havings to go

4.27

(The one disappears then others
At uncertain points leave-taking
Ache of that arm that face gone
Sat outside a lifetime seemed
Numb shock of ~~not~~ everything stopped
Millions of moments fitful tracings
Parts of ourselves gone now
Nothing to say or do in the face of
Just to walk around feels wrong
Birds scatter & regather, clouds
Something eats the seeds to live
The ache has a pulse, is one
No way not to be utterly changed
Beloved face no more to be seen)

4.29

Spasms of motion, molecular doubt
Fusion-musics, what is elegant
Creation's name, a kelson of
Always becoming but writing stays
This was thinking skin in time
Limited intervals but something living
Kept on spattering lightning rain
Curious human animal sometimes pain
A thing in a chair in between-space
Phrases maybe vacancies continual
Place to stay while moving on
Go out in vain come back again
One day the noise was music
Rhythm of night-thought saying
Identity uncoiling toward dawn
The noise was music saying sound
A speech-mouth please & company
Thought is always talking or *is* is
But no more now for now alone
Like having a black eye at the opera

4.29

Externalizations of spring
Moon usually rather affable
String-accompaniment, woodwinds
The marvel of a glass face, flecked
Logic is radiology, insight
Ears, nostrils, unusually open
Space no longer bites & hurts
Clusters of young scatterings
Wingéd purposes, feathered vectors
Nothing says nothing twice
Faint loving constant light breeze
Motions of grace just warm air
Sirens in any distance timely
Passage of beings through space
To have had a friend, companion
In any weather anyway
Bonds between things in time
These gestures, these moist marks
Skin thinking gentle
Hard not to, tiny far kisses
A few faint early late stars

5.1

An art moves roomier, then rain
Soft ticking everywhere plashes
Here is almost-still air, cubits of
Clear anemone on table-top, chairs
Where sight has unseen roots
Who cares to hear a tattered
Psalm beyond page, afterimage
Loved one from other torn
Unfortunate event-turns eventually
Our nervous systems tenuous threadings
Only sense in saying going
We breathe a definite
Animal companion listens perhaps
Body whispers outside images
Some kid's cold ears hear a snowfall
Through enormous silence small, disappears
Whoever could really prepare for
Already someone else
Surrounds, a flurry of unclear
A confusion of clarity-faces, all that
Sure we were knowing, known
The phone checked & rechecked, knowing
What mattered so much at the time
While rain, while nervous systems, names
The already-gone, the going on
The care it takes to place someone

5.1

Outside is anywhere according to reading
You could hide things in a book, skin-bound
Smelled like a foreign country, older
Human organisms could grow there
Told-things, opens, daylit remains
To connect the bright dots between persons
Rivers & runoffs too, changey snakings
In jail the reading was on the walls
Broken things, mouth-parts, bitten hands
The coffee & food always an adjustment
A collapsible area for visitations, chairs
And a paper swamp, so many projects
Pure nothing-music sometimes too
One said you can read my skin see
Products on metal shelves spotless
A picture on a wall a real world
Stale air always stories anyway
The thicker the better to hit with
Thunderstorms elucidate power
At night the walls sweat trickles
And what is luminous supposedly prayer
Maybe no hope but also no permanence
Crouched, we get hidden into the story

5.2

Always a weave of voices always was
And weather, ornithological drifts
Under the overpass temporary shelter
People stop to take their pictures
Each an undertow in a too-small cage
Animal spatter on granite figures
Yet a smell of human longing pervades
The rest of the novel unreadable
Still we synthesize proteins, speeches
A dwarf star bespeaks red giants
These sea-somethings walk the wide water
Museos in whorled shells, coral forests
Bronzed bodies pass by on wheels & sails
A particularly juicy incident then
Tinged with burning gold blue unfurled
Elsewheres half-asleep, buoyed
Even the proverbial birds unruffled
Quilled suggestions of voice, flight
Salt air circulates, a few thin strays
The almost-features of a looked-for face
Curious upwardturned expectant head
Then the rest of our lives occurred
A hive of voices both living & dead

5.2

What suffices is a simulation
A spider has eight points of view
Fewer than six degrees of separate
Unedited volumes twilight letters
Blurred persons in hindsight
We listened with open eyes
Most things no-one witnesses
Swallow a glimmer or murder
An idea in the form of a gasp
Stories are unusually telling
World unearthed with afterglow
We come & go like focused ants
A history of trees writ in water
One solitude stepping around another
Brains on the pavement ungathered
A list, a tourniquet, a telos
Life-raft on the side of a mountain
Gunshots somewhere nearby just now
The radio faint xylophone notes
Violence made the frame anyway
One thought doesn't *follow* another
Young worms rooting under flowers

5.3

To open a moment's noticing
Nothing violent in a shiver
These jellyfish feel pleasantly
A pentapod is not a greeting
Spring jumps from drop to drop
Light will age a window
Neurotransmissive more or less
Filaments between whereabouts
Watermarks, faded epics
Small awkward animal being born
Facticity amid slick grassblades
Again without conclusion
A life reordered instantly
Dumped contents of a desk drawer
Your arm an image of the mind
Movement a fluid medium
The sink clogged with hair
Evenings caught in a tree
Place was when nuance
Turned up hidden routes
Life-forms in the surround
Caverns of nocturnal activity
A green home no figment
Pigments unimaginable outspread

**TIME PASSES

5.15

Moveless clouds, almost pink.
A city lights up distance from distance.
Drops speck, plink, listening.
Moisture gathers, a surface to it.
Almost isn't rust or placement.
Night's all shade over here.
Up one wall small blue lights.
Flat wood along a floor.
Like a hand not moving
Specks, glistens, dustward, movings
Nothing violent or careful at present
Surface tension, droplet, perfect circle
Hangs, which were little dependings
A city of circlets intercollected
The frame changes touch
But don't tell that to the falling
Long wet bent black feather

5.15

In case of animal emergency
Amulets mustn't be neglected
Weather is readable entropy
Along a softness fingers hum or purr
Patchwork of sentences, lives
Entryway between feet & hands
At a moment's notice
Stains on some undone gauze
A blink in behaviour is all
The patterns on the wall cease
Being is born down here to do
There are voices who whisper
Say maybe an inch above the grass
The living outsides of unliving things
A brain made transparent for study
Possibility itself gelatinized lucid
We're it, beyond all games
Cells on a surface instanced
Voice the most various touch
The tendril of this instant curls

5.15

What is is enough for this
Thought where dividedness opened
Mutabilities serve for star-maps
Spread a few faint floor-lights
Pattern an answer to how
Opposing ends sewn together
Stitched into different time-frames
Nevertheless observable
Bodies involute crepuscular systems
Abstractions physicalized, cilia, roots
Night crawling wet intelligence
An audible spreading in difference
Memory is photons & rain
Always a mass of sticks beside us
Hold a quintessence in your hands
Voices of sunset voices of twilight
Throats neither begin nor end
Like pulling a pocketwatch from air
Tall tree full of forms glistens
Glad rather to be unnoticed
A purpose may be kissed or torn
All just one falling feather fallen

5.16

Bodies starved for bodies
Whatever ends
Why always long grass, fields
Meetingplace occasions
Incisions deep & clean
People screaming for material
He cut off his nipple
A gift in the future tense
Pale grey moth can't fail
Tissue strains, places shifty
Faces starved out their eyes
Here was as ever
Day drops down behind
Your door to a river
Whatever wavers
A blur above ripples
Yet a product of façades
So pain, that broken arm
Life of particulars
Indescribable smell of air
Of wet night air
In & out of nostrils' mouths
If not here then where

5.16

Not a transcription of thought
Place produces, a locus opens
You only have to move the known
Matter breathing thinking matter
Your companions are space & air
Somewhere to sit unmolested
Leaf-stillness at the moment, say
Decisions are wired, sequential
Straight from the gift-horse, say
Human aggregates, fuzzy maths
This part of earth presently sleeps
Quiet intersections molecular
A roar of events somewhere
Darkness palpable, densities of trees
Speech might have been kind
A description of stillness passing
Night-quiet in & out of mouths
Some crouch down in the hiddens
Neither nowhere nor somewhere
Far sound constant maybe trains
Easy to see what any night is
Occasionally a stray cat creeps
Birds wake before a world begins

5.16

Any whisper any falling feather
The temporal a retelling
Attention thistled a distance, dawn
Clothes are always afterthoughts
We came crying hither
A body in space-time flailing
Blur of arms & eyes & hair
Mind's in the canal, the conduit
A sunrise ringed with bird-bones
Rhythm arranges gestural day
We're intersections, root-mesh
Neurons cannot feel pain, why repeat
Safety in numbers, sudden rains
And gradually light returns to the street
A recognized face, focused iris
Perhaps the terms are germinant
Suggestion changes lenses, click
Soon noon's all tongues & teeth
Easy to be graphic when visible
Anybody stretches long & curving
Usually in rooms it is said

5.17

Slow, continual cloud-drift
No wind no leaf-flutter
Enormous distant city-hum
Most lead lives of work & home
Simple phrases floated wisps
Things said & done in passing
Small animal slinks quiet
Garbage in proper containers
Most prone asleep in beds
Deepest part of night so-called
No birdcalls yet, no outspread
Mesh of sounds & momentum
Still occasional engine noise
Silence an almost audible ringing
Description next to nothing
Neighbors' TV on all night
Blue light over unhappy bodies
A cure for every ailment
Surplus of comforting fictions
Meanwhile a raccoon
Nimble digits through trash
Sustenance from the betweens
At least enough to go on awhile

5.21

Looking up through the sidewalk
Ripples in the visible, while foot-traffic
All are underlings, specializing day
Some few together-moments made
Secret of durable figments
Pink throated tongues, rubber stamps
Unfold the note with unfolding hands
Wide world-web, semi-celestial spiders
Clouds of flies, communicants, lively
Magpies, curtain calls, far cries
Beneath the meat was something realer
Whispers night & day of betweens
Lines of erratic flight across sunset
Fluid suffusions, final remarks, quietly
Once removed from where you were
A zone of open, but not to eyes
Transmissible, no matter the weather
What we do in lieu of speech
Air-kiss an erstwhile emptiness
All those times you, or when we, they
Just bodies in time as ever
Matter of atoms & memory & red-shift
A few blue lights out over the lake
We live in the wake of what is

5.23

Voices of what, ringworms & dovetails
The tongue no protrusion, a tip
Lips slightly open in twitchy sleep
Green evenings deepening still
Carve a family from the warm air
Memory a coin thrown into ripples
What was was something else
Someone shouting in the street
We're never merely one many
Lives of the days of the branching years
Called to listening & speaking listening
Sound an outpost, a weathering shed
The framed lake, flexible mirror
Dirt was neither curtain nor door
Some choose to go in fire
We coordinate with specialists, alert
Born astride a mirrored grave
Lose a self or two in sound of waves
Day may fade but night might not
Pale festival, no end in sight

5.26

Before-dawn a crawlspace, a between
Doors align us with the known
Warm green breezy centerless
So many so proud & certain
Now night freedom of movement
Someone roots through the discardeds
Still later stray animals friends
If just a mouth could speak
Pins to set a bone, keep place
A time to have a storm of answer
Feather-paths through thought-forms
Dawn the opposite of a bruise
Who would rejoin the wind & rain
Bright all external within
Light without eyes, the skin-face
These steps lead down to where
Old movement of one-to-one, feelingly
Shoots of nerves fanning out forever
So many persons, their importance-machines
All equal in the ground, as ground
Oldest song not for tears
Ashes & water & memory no matter
All finally one, no kingdom needed

12.8

When bodies are wideopen possible
A dream coming from the dream-hole
Somethings written on a wall colorful
A jumble of then & now however here
Also harms they do to one another
Not constant but almost always
To reduce a risk of harm in painting
Image-speech was the wall-purpose
Our insides live inside other insides
There had to be acts of kindness
Always coming back to, or shelter
Hope was called a form of rain
Any skin could be soothed somehow
The rest was mostly breathing
It didn't mind abstraction, peopled
The air a circulatory system clearly
A smallest touch & faintest smile
Outside windows days begin grey-blue
Cannot be meaningless, part of matter
Human body arms wide across daytime
Saw it once dancing actual spastic joy
Beyond walls & clocks & skins & dancing
Still talking, there's hidden, & going on

12.13

Living language come from a terminal tongue
Sound a body branching from surrounds
Usually signal fires either at twilight or dawn
Say a landscape that crags 'til horizons
The whisper of little whiskers on a wrist
Our digits touch the daily in so many
So many bodies set to motion by clockwork
There will not be harm in growth outside this
Night can open so much wider than thought
What survives is human & natural movement
Amid the melted plastic & team players
There is still touch of tongue to other
Not forever the burnt & torn terrorized bodies
Roots of any tongue so much older than speech
Soon a kind of light on & through a window
The transparent possible however unclear
Thumb-smudges on the morning sparrows
Some of our changing faces will continue
Can't find another way to tell the light

1.4

Any mind will do
Where to continue to begin what was
Hums from a terminus
And small once-green lifeforms border
Any off & on is machinery
Once a year one sits here
Plus-strokes from position nada
Yet there must be tides, stomach-linings
In frozen soil still living worms
Chair view through a window
Trickles may turn recursive
From averages, from human scenery
Any oily spectrum from a gutter
Before freezing whiteness sets in
A body covered in cloth or not
Fabric gathers moisture
Hopeful woven seems tough
A life gives off heat, invisible radiance
The gloves still glow awhile, & foottracks
Form is an animal of sorts
Any touch can tell
It all only seems to stop
An outpost inside hearing knows

1.4

A curtain made of eyelashes & glass beads
This time of year we mayst be cold
Though it's quite very rare in dreams
All the eyelashes on earth at the moment
Just before & then as dawns begin
Dim air become very slightly blue
Then bluish-grey the rest prehistory
While a black cat washes with long pink tongue
That town of fear where air grows old
So many red memories along iron rails
Neither a follower nor a fucking buffoon be
The long glass girl gets stoned alone at noon
No spoils only a bunch of dumb victors
We're trained to be afraid by monsters
Jocular the voice while quite pinched the face
Forms of human suffering hurrying to & from
Yet a new species or three just now or soon
The seed goes down, sod dies, then boom
A frozen pinnacle revolves, icy silences
A terrible feudalism is born, tuberous, warty
Songs to itch that itch that itches & longs
A sentence with basilisk skin says twitches
He spun a world on one finger then split

1.5

Music so like day-noise you can hardly
The voice changes voices no discernible
Smell of mortality yes & stale deodorant
Or teeth & hair, eyelids over rose-petals
Beyond snow is nowhere momentarily
Whereas here a night chatters
Intertwistings, strands of colored wall-lights
The thinking strands
Where hope is toothmarks on a book's spine
Ad imitatum
An underskin prickly with potential energy
How some things linger
Remains among
Loved one gone, the rest stuck ongoing
Maybe filaments of daytime braided with night
You have at least three believable bodies
One has quartz eyes, calmly
Signal-fires still burning miles from here
While some are forced into shelters or cages
Children nearby love those blue lights
Then a sign where a mouth was
Some nights the cold is crystallized clarity
Must remember nature knows no malice
Jokes slow down in snow, mouths slow
A baby born with parts of another extruding
Not even granite's set in stone

1.5

Another tree thrown, same lawn
Nothing doing
Born into what newness
Cathedral windows, light stains, gravities
Occasional animal companion
Two patterns passing across landscape
City a readable accretion, quickness
A torso is not a time-piece
Yet the head screening
Grass waits, fingers under, mumbles
Pain is no system to pointing
Glass can be thought neither living nor dead
The sight of motion refracted
What gathers who
Any stick of the mass distantly
Meanwhile quasars
No compendium, no moment-amber
The kid protected his dead brother's footprint
We're refracted through other lives
Other dust
Being but a trick of light in air
Nothing falling, wind just below zero
Windows smeared with before & after
One returns
Bones are only inwardness
Exhalations, moist ghosts, must rise

1.7

Mind's in the fireplace
Writing on the walls
A play of corpuscles in sun
Which way in a vacuum
Came saying mobilized air
None announcements
Bright winter midnight streetlight
Some passageway through listens
A joke is mobilized pain
Arrived at act three we must
Passage through a body
A god digesting snow
Moments ago have aged change
Departures flown birds quit
Your premises sprout hairs
Whereas & so on knowing
Winter slows liquids possible
A bracelet of bright hair
And zero at the known
One goes on doubling awhile
Tree projected on windblown tree
A then in blizzarded now

1.7

Rooteds, vegetable glass, lucids
The rain has not remained rain
Unreal worlds turn rarely
Little ideational insects assist
Patterns in our afterthoughts clearly
Underground, cunning, fundament
·One urinates a name in snow
New glasses make a new face
The remains of the way unclear
Mercury storm on mirrory seascape
Still children crecend
Analogies to plant life absurd
What is human becoming
Thought that can thinks itself
Fourth dimensional entity in three
Shoveling the mostly frozen driveway
Paradise wasn't built in a day
The cat three-&-a-half dimensional
Obviously the imperceptible
Or hairs on the rim of the toilet
Creatures are mostly appearance
Varied rhythm in cellular structure
Selves leave holes in the nothing

1.8

Neither dark nor light no answer
Night however within without
We move along amid surface
Throat-song in a far corner
Or some kid playing with time
Removals, new uses, stretched youth
Butterflies raised behind bay windows
The glass of a face, portrait-self
Parts of ourselves gone then
A chatter of culture, smeared lens
Azure hath a canker
Daily nightly recital violence
The assailant wore a face or faces
Points of view reshuffled by
Amid a thousand blind windows
Who matter what speaks
These are the days that wore her eyes
And by no man this recursus
Neither from nor toward, no wonder
Thisness, winter stasis, blown husk
Unmemorables, deep quiet, dust
Freezing music, bodies gone dumb
There was a world, it had a moon

1.27

That time that day
Infected memory warmly
Young ones off to school
Those faded speckled
On your walking shoes again
What morning occasion
Man under bridge lives
Traffic-people incompletely push
Only snowfall ceases
Reasons, accumulations
Pattern on a teacher
Careful with careful hand
Small space between ribs
For the remainder of
Music freezes music
Face bathed in blank
Light was what remembered
To enter that clearing
Humane intact alert
Sound of water maybe rain
Listening infinitely careful fingers
For the rest of
Lips & eyes intact
A careful focused blinking
Orifice through & through
Voice glossed over after
Suffer the little
What was always
Not to mind saying

Where loosens & lengthens
Twilight through canal-gaps
Tricklings lengthening widens
What will have out
All thought greened gone

1.27

Welcome to the entertainment center.
Please keep both hands on the screen.
Yes. Next some meaningful music.
Doubt's a phantom. This is the life.
A space of infinite possibility, yes-yes.
Here's a hologram of a young pigeon.
Everything's included in your initial fee.
That's right, let it all out; right.
No, most of history hasn't happened yet.
You sound just like your old self then.
That rainbow-spume is one summer's end.
A fiction protects your neck & head.
Minding gaps is the most one can do.
A truism a day keeps monotony in play.
And now for some very fine syrups.
May you evolve into your own avatar.
These webbings come highly recommended.
Fate's made of photons. Feel that kiss.
Bells & whistles, grins & frowns, O yes.

1.28

Not an irritable reaching after
Always a body where
Burnt silhouette in brown grass
One went one way
Name written on winter air
Dark doesn't hurt, it licks
Mind lives by the canal
Down in where water weeds
Ten sensible fingers twitchy
Some of these citizens judge
Who climbs a column of air
Weeds, leaf-layers trampled, bedding
Branches an endless bifurcations
Disguise grew from the face
Interwovens, thatch-words, lattice
From there to nerve-ends, sputum
Two split lips, muddied outlet
Found an old pile of new clothes
Spider-home, spiralled hallways
Violence keeps the seasons
Who was meaningful in leaves
Parts blurred in the burning
Stagger amid the unfinished
Ashes to reach after anyway

1.31

Another night another mind
Temperature oddly elevated
For this we are
A door in the open closed
A skinful of thimbles a harmful of farms
Body turns blue from falling
To hold openness out, whap
Arms elongated thin crags the horizon
A single multitudinous peaked & caved
What was saying doing
Collected life-forms here-swarms
Pause in the street say to let the clouds
And crowds of time thriving
This one & that one the struck mirror
Mosses crop up on circumstance
To find a translucent wherewithal
It wasn't even all difference now
Smooth cool lake-face still
Thought shot through a prism
A refracted limb ripples
Signs are with your wiles then
Blue bouquet of fingers
Or a mouth for blistery hole
A longing moves lightly breezes
Two shadows play on a swing-set
Don't we go somewhere in sleep
Stone steps mostly unattended
Grey bird's body, shelter of glossy
Way to go in & through falling wet

2.4

A door to the farm & when
Whistling, fields of thistles & vines
Privacies of dilapidation
The pace of rust, furrows in the cyclic
Blue fox beneath foaming moon
Skinned body in spasm backwards
Discolorations beyond its tips
One's one friend cannot
A mind congealed on pine-boards
Occupied a time
Moss tells the way then
Hearings, knot-holes, old story
Can't seem to expand the lungs
A sentence is precipitate
Put mercury in a furnace
One friend is extrafluorescence
None wanted such sputum this
Children dizzy for a piece of plastic
The wire-mouths aching holes
Sunset mottled with drizzling blisters
The running forms, naked, something
A material world altered immaterial
Yet rhythm inhuman persistent
The gristled fizz of language
Torso-thickness, ozone-smell
Tell of the taste of that time
What failed to become, stumped
Jumped still rooted to a chair
Where numb touch turned a page
Scatter of unwanteds, fresh dead X
Forced to be ongoing again

2.4

It stands to reason
Numbers caked with frozen mud
History a lived asymptote
A ragged plastic transparence billowing
Between was here & what'll
Shuttled to & from occupations
Deodorized shadows focused hairless
A trillion insects will inherit
Some cryogeny, some digitized whimper
An instinct for disowning instincts
Bodies torn apart by unknowing
This one feeds on that one's children
Difficult to say what anyone
And how ragged plastic flapping
Or the two kids fucking during gym
Small hollow remarkable sunset
Adults screaming about adults screaming
Goldfish boils in tank, or boredom
Graffiti on the face of pain
Pointy skin of staples & tacks on a pole
Touch is the last to go
And what is called drowning music
A last world keeps spasming
Just add the blood & doubt
A few little ashy circles in the weeds

●

[To have put a buried life away
In where ground, open to snow
Traffic passing no matter backdrop
Final privacy forty feet from paved
Smallbody carried across, stranger
Forelimbs light-colored extend from towel
Nest of protective stick-clutter near
Two arms care, only carrying here
Peace be you now, nameless
Privacy of open woods & pure weather
Courage carried you across the road
Scared, though our oldest task on earth
So we don't die among garbage
You may deepen & unfold, silence
Only ticking unfrozen drops pure
No way to say how you are, home.]

3.2

One human animal said to another
Or jokes about the weather which
We had to have a clean set, stainless
The bodies arrayed, coins & eyes
A dirty carnation taped to a stick
March wind, a seizure in the street
Election shouts, one vomits confetti
Turns out his hair a security helmet
A rage of cornfields, borderlands
Fear of the other-colored face
To have brought a species to this
A joke a monumentally savage
To have burned & greed & stolen & hatred
The news a series of giddy bloodlets
Passed out, frostbite took both legs
We were evicted from shitholes
Who cried in the fucking street
The seizure of all this one day no more
The human experiment managed to murder
Still a gazelle flies from a lion where

3.3

Then a softening in the general turmoil
That candle also
Bacterial constellations, useful blooms
Snow falling almost sideways now
This year really no weather whatsoever
A man in a boat lacking a lake
No analogy for mind, faux morphology
Useful rootings-down only phrases
They tore a child out of a book
Brain can't make its own cries
There was sound in a river, bright turning
To remember life from within it
Duration's name, erosive possibles
The face of things frozen now, clocked
A little moment-by-moment trail to the wall
Some made a hive of jangled laughter
Weeds from the brake where we played
A form in the air magnanimous
How do you carve a tree
Two-cent comments, not everyone's violent
Little quivering light very late at evening
The broken where we play with strays
Small soft head amid wild flowers
There could be there was there had been
An hour or three for dried flowers
Who to touch these days for a shiny
Even a slight relaxation to dawn

3.3

Body-smells, organs settle, rooms
All the simultaneous bipeds on earth
This side of things folded in mostly sleep
Somewhere someone drowning now, has
From under, you can't hear where
At one point there were so many places
Intimacy with insects, roadkill, refuse
Proximity of molecules & orifice
Now is where meetings hold
People galvanized by violence done to others
Hallways, remains, bracelets of bright hair
However lost, harmed, however changed
A face still a face when under topsoil mulch
Or warm ashes, upswirls, settle by ones
A cult of personality with no membership
Live sailor under the blue sea screams
Anemone-wavelengths, mental meetings
Two birds fucking in the crotch of a tree
The tongues of things, beads of eyesight
A brain has no name, nor face nor hair
Nextdoor an animal relaxes, attuned
Something comes out spidery mindwise
Mostly just rhythm murmuring away
Thought furnishes its parts toward
Sliced everyway came into being
What to do was elsewhere said & done
Small animal taking wide road chances

3.30

A few warped boards, slivered minutes
Or a long thin slice of sun in a numbered room
The robots who sang our songs were agreeable
After this sign or that what was thinking then
Grey book, red weather, green dawnlets
Chemical vectors in a bloodstream
To have genuinely at root lost one's way
Day can eat like maggots all at once
Even the terms ache unworking sit
You're only you if your little dog knows it
Any number in fact of hopefully animals
Any body in a chair in time or stands
Limbed shadow as the day is long
All sense of adventure will be back after lunch
No-one said that skittering noise skittered
An abstraction sliced by a kitchen knife
The parts are skinned wonders, moves
Who went away & elsewhere returns
And some voices lost & some won
A body in pain stops asking its name
Some were called sundown & some eclipsed

3.31

Night is know-how looked at sideways
Anything strung along a treeline leaning
Voices, human & non-, multiply divides
Clouds move faster nearer now, fainting pinks
A pet mouse plays on an aging knee
A sentence is no explanation, looked at only
Cops made them put the greeting cards away
Purpose & blisters & movement so
To get something going like fire from treesmoke
Most arrangements predicate a center
Among the eventuals, vitals, virtuals, entrails
Motion of an arm through air means here
Spent her days gluing third eyes on ceramic fish
She was the maker of both eyes & fish
Glue-guns, fusions, skins camera'd
Tubular bells, smart video pets, leprosies
And for the rest of that winter vacation
We gather in corners then storm out
Silent avalanche of nonoccurrence
To keep on turning up at the roots like this
Where blank dry sky finally arrives, used

4.3

Songs of inertia, plastic tubing, masks
A child's a thread wound around wire
Someone said fire from the pretty mouths
Doubt would be less clean in time
A long stick could touch such limits
Whose crumpled conformed quiet bodies
Mother in a larger vehicle drives children
The day is to & from work & street & home
Optimal, netted, supersized, chattery
Spattered hereafters on an alley wall
Some of this still depends on real-world thinking
Extending only so globally as we can throw it
Here are holes between the heaves
The tearing of teeth & hair out, dead air
A pricey veneer festooned with newsfeed
Human thing become its trivial sputtering
Yet money & factories & ideological
No wonder a rage at lack of wonder
So many busy trying to shit out their own shadows
Why would tribe need be dominant reality
The group-think team-sport costly glitter
You were so splattered after no time to plink
And real ones were harmed & burned & covered
Soon away to hell & out of there, done

4.4

A hole in dark or some other superstructure
Tunnel up through under there widens
To a million tiny holes in childhood
Averages, rough-hewns, light thickens
Cathedral of weeds, droplets of attention
Or later like a cave inside of hearing
Not all of these beings shout
Standardized twists & turns, departure-points
You could crawl to amazement as often as not
Starlings, barn owls, swallows, redspecks
Heat had circulatory problems as often
Some lay in wait too for walking
Lots got torn though quieter nights
Undersides, hiding, insect against glass
Coming & going & covers & leaves
Sidewalk diamonds, a painted moth, stains
On a present tense whereabouts then
That one staggering, streetlit snow
We are revisited by sticky continuals
'Til there's no we, no harm, no holes

4.4

Snow somewhat yellowy streetlight
No traffic only faint hum
Wires from the back of a head
Radio an endangered species, print
Unexamined organs, perceptual receptacles
The mind a terrible thing to taste
Spattered onto frozen sidewalk grass
Still children get excited about
But who would go on knowing
Reduced to stuck kinesis in streets
A slow yellow not even urinous
Flat, chemical, leeched, static noncolor
'Til soon large vehicles
And some kind of enormous metal scoop
Wearings-away of material on material
Days filled with digits & purpose
Transparent overlay plus skin-masks
Unnumbered corpses gathered & ordered
As actual animals skirt the center
At least then sense organs dilate
All cervical, factual, poised, damp

4.6

Story of quiet of betweens
Heart of, something of
Left something on vibrating rails
A tissue-thin monotone
Or an overpass collapses killing
Suffusions of news of wires
No more ticker tape time
Thought records backwards
Rabbits in the backyard dew
Here stillness passes slow
And three kids kicked out of college
On a tip, iceberg'd, a later matrix
Fuse burnt out behind wood
We displace air rearrange dust
Rust is lively, timely, fervent
Our machines & clothes to-be-laughable
Jawbones of an ass, durables
Really in an animal loop
A time to torture & a time to maim
Ground into glass-dust, grit
Hacked at, tongues uprooted, stript
Crimes continual, shellacked with thought
While a ragged man buys scratch-offs
Two quiets, we are all between

4.6

All sleep, all still, something hums
Can a mind   farther than the street
Neither Winter nor Spring
Terms of germination, insects-to-come
Transparent but material limbs, feelers
Hast thou an arm of fire
Or had to hold in a scream
So the porchdoor slams, it rains, snows
Nobody knows
A kid in a well swallowed a key
Told him to act bravely, nationally
Repeated blows to a growing head
No-one asked what's good
The ground a permanence of sorts
Rhizomes, tendrils, weeds are even
Coordination of the muscles of a face
Everybody so busy doing
There were eyes & hair & teeth then none
Stream said not to mention
And a camera in the backroom
Like a witness to the gristle
Exposure negative develops
Minds are wired, violence writhes
Later something's still, still later
Backyard stars a gift, cold blessing
Gentle survived a little, was the trouble

4.10

A succession of heads mouths busying
Well-trained functionaries, bladders on sticks
Or you grew up to be beat by the thing
The talking sticks, the belonging-pile
This wasn't even thinking anymore jumbled
Only burned homes, hacked cheekbones, & such
Such a rotted intricately inward-twisting
Spattered with expensive toys & pseudoscience
As if bones weren't real except as means
To consume the pain & folly of daily others
Jokes around the watercooler, absence of air
Absence of watercooler, neutralized carpet
Consuming something through ear-buds
The pelvis the genitals mostly inert, codified
People screaming over the terms of identity
Belonging-screams, privilege-screams, bordered
Endless debates about meaningful
Sign says no swimming here, a problem
The finding out softness, silky fluidities, plashes
There are no wires in water, only under & over
Human contact happens in movies too
Pliant screens, depth fields, eventfulness
They pulled his torso-skin up over its head
When torture stops it doesn't end
Violence come to speak through you instead

4.10

The tongue part of the brain
Lives on its own anyway
The taste the smell of spring air
Pink spongy muscle, haired nostrils
More like underwater organs
A body talks to itself at night
Paralyzed force despite twitches
Smell of a sense of something missing
The way rain may soon feel
In time the mind thickens patterns
Ridiculous animal in clothing
Called to witness its trivia
These think money power things
Yet some still must
Acts of mind in art alive
Not shackled to cause & effect
Otherwise commodity pain example
A trying to find, this please, when
The gift's the thing itself

4.13

Rest is relative motion constant
Avenue seen through unfoldings
A haze of lives burned from earth
Broken hip in Springtime's fusions
Small ones huddled in eternity
Green guesses at the meanings of
Wonder possible even on TV
A child of four dimensions sullen
Phosphorescences over an ocean
New moon a hot commodity
Now & then sprout futures
Fingernails begin to undercurl
Patrol vehicle missing a hubcap
Some drunk kid died at the game
Is that placeless, to be left
A kind of photosynthetic prayer shawl
Birdfeather necklace, bone amulet
Smooth the uses digits find
He was wiry, liked to stay up later
They called it just a minor war
Live awhile we above ground
Now the moon, sun, rain, cities
The sound of openings closing
Flexible plastic & wires for an arm
Microchip embedded in the unfeeling

4.24

Had to use a match to read his watch
Small arc of scar tissue on an arm
Persons unknown yet networked by signs
Out over the lake some weird bright crescent
Wind in & out of the picture went through
We're frames in which time leaves a moving image
One novice unfolded a map & made for cover
Horror was a mass of sticks moved nearer
Still children's voices in imaginary gardens
The fact is the sweetest dream labour
But these dummies keep muttering judgments
An abstraction whispered stickily in your ear
Clearly the mouth a kind of ear too
Water tables, mental diadems, mossy clocks
The hills are alive with the sound of fusion
One meditates, one masturbates, one runs
The air & how to get there beyond confusion
From the first something fulminating
A broken thinker, brightpale greydreaming meat
Complexities aren't always inedible
A suffusion of reference-frames kept us warm
Shell-whorls, specks of flight, excrescence
Still on a neck a kiss can do good
Assuming another century'll hold off awhile

4.24

Opened up the body found dried flowers
Out toward where flickering warm returns
And when dangles down to moisten roots
What else to think but bodies in time
The sales pitch, gradient, greased wheels
Certain congealed terms bandied about
Yet we had high hopes for the positron
Though airports leery over titanium crania
That day lunch in the museum was fun
Nature a vast green million-limbed conspiracy
He wore a glass donkey mask to petting zoos
Impossible to return the presence now
A numb tongue can be a stressful sign
To return a curtain to an obsidian cube
Perfecting one's grasp of the language of the dead
In winter wonder after getting over briars
Plainly yours is an overwrought sarcophagus
And cracked lips the mouths murmur further
Why the human accident why asking
Those are hills that were her thighs
Delicious to have touched soft down succulent
Still-smouldering radiating fusioning body
To ache for a real dream feels freedom
Mind on fire with desire another other
So we are not merely angry selfimportant trivia
Endless weird languages of the unending body
A spectrum enfleshed, spasms of radiant thought

4.24

Same bunch of mummies, same damn tomb
What's simple plus a dirty window
Grime of fact times time pressure
To coordinate, see how many show up
Under the pup tent, shiny medicinal flyers
Free food will convince things of people
A gorgon screamed at a college student
Officially fire cannot be a symbol of anything
Kept his dreams under lock & key in a funnel
One wonders is torture still *in* this season
Those steps lead up to where they went
A mouth doesn't speak to anyone's mouth
Who's burning, & different tissues, bounds
Two nervous systems walked home alone
These beings, two homelessnesses, histories
Or candidates made of nonhyperintelligent plastic
And sun & moon & tree vibration please
In all their loneliness & pain & years
To at least indulge in madspeech for
Poor bare forked & so-on howling yours
Though at times like kissing a kitten in the belly
There are still infinitely gentle mental acts
All this written on water in a grotto, O
Naturally the hollowness is key

4.27

Afternoons spent describing circles, arcs
The not-yet-echoing green greens
Something many-appendaged warm coming
How even dust smells different whirls
Any animal seeks warmth is safety
From a turret two grey balloons uptwist
Man in blue glasses with talkative hair
Coilings of spring into boilings of summer
Absurd the terms distinguish gradients
Always was meanwhile & therefore as
Any shiny little thimbleful of violence
Some drunk in a furnace, girl in a gulch
While nations barred from being nations
So many soundless drowning in paper
Frozen blood cut up into cubic portions
If the eye were an animal
Suburban exterminators, merit badges, rage
Still a kind of cold fire, root-life spreads
When upward lilts a sentence as
Green vectors begun, time grows visible
Soon again the sun illimitable dominion
Yes only briefly punctuated by nights

4.29

First birds, their sounds, in any case
Two minutes ago were night
Cold enough to be a living beginning
First sounds, in any case, follow
A lively understandable spirit once
Any presence companionates & forms
These figures both places & gestures
The living form subdividing groans
While others go gambling on a cruise
Always the human body coming going
A wealth of always in a wash of never
The back wall of the eye become a husk
With after-messages for the before
All equal in sleep pretenses shed
A mind crying backwards in time groans
Weeping sore of a divided self
Like a root they pulled a kid from the soil
With one symbolic earthquake in his eye
A spider tells no-one about something
Dawn birds complex communicative systems
Why not be proximate to semantic webs
The temporal indivisible from the physical
When time doesn't pass we're it

4.29

Language neither afterthought nor lens
That evening was an awkward simile
This mask comes with monocle, flap of hair
Laughter bypasses cerebra
For this we are & cut portions of us
For the absent friend who swam down air
At the end of a hallway a muffled cough
Falling down time always eventuals
Spread the redolent guts out on trays
Magic glitter, a puff of dust, toy books
Particles of each inevitably remain
The tongue was damage, from damage
Not some mere information transmitter
What did you think a mouth was for
What think the motley language from
Though we are only folds in a material
Something moved on the waters vast
Down daily conflagration uprushing remains
One said I was hardly among you
How participate in human material games
For whatever laughter's for
We're an animal that needs its needs
That much at least is afterthought
Those are abscesses in the laughter's eyes

4.30

Stiff feelers on an ocean floor
Identification must be prominently
How to give out sandwiches, soups
The human organism scanned
An element of blank window
Change of clothes, inflow & outflow
Claimed he could walk through walls
A bicycle journey along highway
Cloud-patterns, local birds, trash
Pebbles arranged around a small curled
Always a knit of identity
Whether cancer or green causality
This canal continues underground
A form of person, archway, door
Physical mysteries down a face-side
That torment's neither water nor air
So many rent from so many others
In humid purple twilight one star
The boy removed his beard & wrote
Rubber eye-holes at the turret's base
A giant insect speaks in phrases
From one spire of the world to another
'Til elevators drop us decidedly down
Somewhere rest outside the mind
There must be truly inhuman

4.30

Body incomplete continuous unfolding
First put the paperwork back in the basket
Lemons are not really part of lexicons
Or waves of outforking vasculature
The thing writhing & turning in sunset
Feeling of palpable endless, a mist of gold
Trained to ride a unicycle under big tents
Stars tattooed on face & crotch, planets
Striated tissues, rainbarrels, X-ray specs
A memory of overalls walked on its own
While the rest of the world angry traffic
The tarantula handler's a philology major
And small chartreuse concepts directly relevant
When only one thermometer for seven families
Bone dice, mysteries made of glass, wax eyes
Seemed there was rough fabric reality
Small girls & boys hoisted onto shoulders
To dream awhile without knowing it
Miracle of matter bodymind unfolding
The illusion that magic is real
Changed change, wider inside than what befell
Lemons part of that lexicon surely
Sour grapes, worn jokes, dead letters
Small container of soup a true gift
And we never planned to be adequately
Remember others already undertowed
Stay awhile where infinite limbs
If anyone were ever kind to any other

5.1

Parts of eternity passed in school assemblies
Assortment of organs some human some not
Long flowing undulations of liquid light
Three spectres leechlike attached to protrusions
Ointments & flies, rodents & camera-angles
Limbs elongated outsprouting limb-blossoms
Rain grey thinkable translucence waves
Ah the vast fertile quiet after human chatter
Here wounds are washed not washed away
Bodies multiplying languages within themselves
Temporarily gelled permanences began an ooze
Material beings in rivering worlds swim
These warm blown rainwaves a reasoning force
Streets & subdivisions of a minute order
So many tiny activated pasts quavering
One says leechlike though moreso anemones
Green naturally included extensible frame
Nothing petty or greedy undulations
Mounds, domes, geometry always insectile
Apogee-branches glistening outward reach
As whole spectral populations spring
All included in the living breathing frame
The spatialized eternal its fecund seconds
As physical propulses extraphysical

5.1

Audience removed by forceps, precepts
A blonde kid skinned his knees
Another she maybe bit another's lip
We are pretty down here in hollows
Sutures movement too
People were excellent waves over there
One ocean-moon a kind of mind
Liquids in & out in any case
An old hand starts to make new marks
Tiny feathered islands dart through air
We displace marks too
And by the side of a wide river calm
A music of normal noises
Not bone grinding bone or tooth removed
Scattered gatherers, chair to strap down in
Hunched listening up
Always the body along waterlines
Trees are background assurances
A small piece of blue was kind
Didn't even require an eye
No sensation in first places imagined
The way to set a bone gets learned
Magnesis, parthenogenesis, vervet verve
Any bone gets learned along water
No way anyway to leave off, remove

5.1

A gold skull with blue glass eyes
Some portion of space opened up
You were as far as you could throw you
Long arch of a spine in timed air
Childhood-way was slower water
As if a portion of the streaming open
Warm door to a river, painted air
No temple system needed to frame
Only what upcrops in endless jungle
Old life poured through green doors
The human frame saturated with radiance
Pouring from its orifices
An older time than metalled worlds
Screech of wheels & factories & wars
Some rust in child-hidden hunching
Warm air whirls up from canopy
The gentle membranes came & went
Body become a mossy understory
Firmly rooted through dust committed
Screaming & laughing & believing
Dawn still that same rubied reckoning
Soft conflagration of the living & dead

5.3

Alone in a kind of night-music
Someone sleeps on an air vent
A full sentence isn't
At least sale prices won't considerably
Glare of nowhere no purchase
Conversation recalled in a dream
Rage is all the new this season
Fungus clinging to our best wishes
Rubber eyes plastic tongues gaggling
Or a girl agog in dandelion time
Planets stream from hands & feet
A suddenness of bright greens blued
Good reasons for webbed feet truly
Wingspan pockets of somethings coming
A hologram for the gold girl breathing
No sense of fear of fear, removes
Bracketed patchwork of red vessels
Eyes in shade then soon in sun
Where blinking, where inwardly
And some of us fail to find air
Despite the tips of the textures of night
No tongue completely sensible
A spiderpath through architecture
The sum keeps slipping from the frame

5.3

For & of no-one
Ceiling fan gently
A face feels is
Uncovered by layer
Dust touched dust just so
Small music far
Minutes proceed at length
A body in a chair as
A long pause in air
No lips or eyes or hair
Where a beginning
Noise of horns
The mind a gap
Not place nor movement
A pain in a finger points
Isn't this all vibrates
Whereas rain or where
Another face or time
One was sitting was
Dust just deus ex'd
Lively understandable
We traced for what
Not passing minutes
Thought mouths

5.3

Some of the world awash in bodies
Ideolects marketplace steel & reaches
Purpose burnt out eyes & ears & tongues
The thirst of a minute or a lifetime
Riverbed message, a bomb in a cooking pot
Three fingers found thirty yards away
Cubist space with thumbtacks thorns
Shreds, schoolroom fear of survival
There are terrorists of the norm too
Hate cuts out genitals & brainstem
All the leaves all a city's trees fallen ashes
One child wanders into a mirror for life
Bodies jerked flailing in pain or numbed
Walking corpses bloated commercials
The impetuous impotent
Self-murder an older option workable
Bird's wing pale yellow rainy sidewalk
Each day to walk from confusion rain
To find fingers in a tree or sunset faded
A kitchen table not a firing range
Average daily dangerous ignorance
Through actual moist sweet spring air
It must be all of a restive piece
Why writhe why not sapling-ache
The rage the writhing the spring air one
All already somehow settled, done

5.5

Three bodies dangle from a bright arch
In televised space blurry grainy
Moneyed furnaces a market stench
Wideopen street, a heard glimpse
Or warm torn midday coverts, passages
Three mapped pins placenames for
Following backwards that this time
No-one uses anymore poles for
Or cruciform, yet still a viral idea
Was not producing specific content
Infused world in a tangle
Who wants to come to a point
Caught the relevance, the groundwork
Furnished sandstorm plexiglass windshield
The thing had to keep organizing signs
Or spitting teeth & hair & eyesight
Reruns in red grassfield, vomit
Ember-smears where someone went
A body thickness smells, gas
Series of more or less spastic gestures
Air a kind of fuel-smelling swirling
At the point of self-expression
Pages & pages wet with drops
Who took the teeth from knowing
While tribal judgment sits
Gilt-framed chair-backed comfort
Bent burnt human forms hang in air

5.5

Maybe almost finished voices changing
Spasms of gesture soon greyblue dawn
Same grave same ticking size of air
Something human pacing cages
Clawed hacking what was thinking
In all that glass a single animal hair
They throw pots & pans in the kitchen
Young boy's head the size of a grapefruit
Any longing is not the other
Quivering visible conflagration sunset
Small grassland animal something shivers
Wind continually picking up above us
All the momentary heads on earth asleep awake
The hair warmth hairlessness of real each, touch
And what if sentences gnarled come
Pouring raging flooding from sense-organs
Two small hemispheres under cranium
Spring & all trees erectile function
Not so much a patchwork skincloth quotations
Only nonabhorred writhing in this vacuum
At least one animal handburied by a river
Sometime roaring on mudways behind you
How many mouths must a nothing need
City town & nation prosthetic temporaries
Jarring when one of the bodies crumples
Always the same very same red river
Ever-recognizable cry one thing for another

5.6

It's anytime outside now hidden
Drifts of bodysmell in leafshape
As if the air budded, tiny unfurlings
Who could think of cages or persons
One long pause between night & day
Chains of interlocked bodies as events
What is this thing inside its skin
What arm is asking the question
We were advised to include a world
A piece of evening, some kid's shoe
Twig-&-leaf bags left out opposite
Across the moisture from here
Slow carlights through the nonmurk
Engine sounds intestinal walls
Our wood-&-glass boxes aloft & un-
A man made a toy man in boxes
Beards may be attached with rubber
One little one had glass eyes
A dog's mouth's well-designed moist
Some other slowcreeping cars gurgling
When they step on a human is angry
Subdividing presences from the sternum
Spatter crackling the rest in spasm
This is not for tears thinking but
Never did anyone do anything other
Than action reaction a rush of breath

5.6

Suppose a pause a pleasant day
The comings & goings going & coming
Say an effulgence from rockface
A small below canal operative fecund
A populace of minnows through narrows
He could turn hands to bird-shadows
Continual slams & honks from machines
Maggots have a noble occupation
Pure transformation, stretched faces of
The wrenched forms of, spastically
Playthings must still for children be
To be strewn across the earthface
Red weather, we drove past cataclysm
Far sirens, reversible time, magma
A friendly entertaining spirit once
Birdfeather collection, dried vertebrae
Semiparalyzed dreaming truncated body
Neurological singularities are legion
Faces to be taken at gift value
A belt of teeth, rusty spigots
Signs stained on a piece of waving cloth
Puppets keep their own secret clubhouse
Everywhere grass & weeds & groundlings
Coffins don't make for containment
Soil will always have its say
So knowing branched limbs that twigged

5.10

A cluster of disappointed presences
Somewhere likely near likely water
The mottled continuance of things as they
A few kids chalking colorful walk
Or stormclouds potentially operatic
Awayturning, secret hiding place
Yearslong perspective narrowing
First rivulets then splatterings
A bright dullness of bicycled streets dims
Weather the most common parlance
One quickness yoked to another slow
Wormsmell, earthbreathing, lushly
Two fundaments sat on a bench
To pause a whisper, pass through noon
Where meanwhile future strangers
Woven in & out of the picture's border
Begin means merely going on
Pigeons occasionally or sparrows, sun
Agitation of tiny beaks for seeds
Droplets, a stitch of rain-shawled
Some metronome maybe in ear-bones
Still the breathing people lean
Breathing & talking & at certain tasks
Sensation itself a pastime when
Maybe something in the water too

5.10

Again & again how now
Through part of a world a sentence
She dropped her cone, sidewalk
The investigator wore antlers
Free agents placed the scene
Some humdrum thrum of fingers
We're constantly risking the movies
Then a large weird man filled the hall
Tear ducts lead to mean labyrinths
Your procedures are enormous
We eat fried dysfunction smiling
Crumpets are probably not objects
Green goblets, tooth-rings, moldy robes
In a forest clearing lo
To dance in wooden circulars
Swing up into the fruitful tree
Conical hats, noonday candles, lunacy
Twelve fingers from a single pale limb
Staggering mad toward the outhouse
Boxes of futile solutions for all
A pole to poke the certain fruit
Scenes of merriment, patterns ripening
Spectres awash in rags of leaves
Sky-portions small upon them
A general up-kicking of hooves
The dance always circular somehow

5.13

Days & nights more appreciably warm
You look up & time's wide
Crosscurrents, transit hubs, humus
There is no body in general
Cricket-grass, fog-cabins, underwear
Or in a city's digestive tracts
Stuffy rooms puffed with fluff
A note on the table, wall in the hall
Formal apparel found unsuitable
Somebody's brains spread out on the table too
Colorful pickings, a crust of emanation
Red hand, plastic fingertips, suckers
To write the real & unreal conglobed
Rain in hollows follows harms gently
At first just a little pinch then
Boxes of rained-out options stored stacked
A child from the lives, from legs & arms
Til the storm came invaginating energy
Some massive multiplier whirling
Dailiness, dull aches, nagging constants
To show us what electric really means
The rest is convenience, mirror-trends
Who to consume digital pellets
Pixellated image of an imaginative fetus
Then an everyone screaming over teams
How survive the mind
No one's home, dog as witness, lessness
One's one friend's friend, for an end
Not even the machinery of poetry & pain

5.13

Genitals touching genitals, pre-dawn
Uncertain slowness of certain quickness
Quiet in the mind, its tips, pinking
Vague gentle warm soothing breeze
Nothing returns or can
Unfoldings of open, then headlights
An animal companion listens
The self not so marketable, remarked
Sometimes sickens mistake, falls
Or seedy, weedy interstices, bother
An inscaped mountainside on fire
In a mostly paper & flower place
And to think that one thóught one thought
Why go on in the ongoing trapped
A spattered vacuum ringed with teeth
A mouth of eyes whatever works
People have such neat & ordered lawns
All the little flowerheads in lightness rain
Skins of an image, nerve-pinch, eye-juice
Nothing really belongs here but dirt
The little puff-birds that bounce the canal
Wander will you from dust to dust
And what is called crime transpires
Angles of rain & ripening, porous plus-signs
Clocks are an endangered species
We become stream-lined personless wetfolds
Still tubes & monitors toward an end
The tatters of an angry family, sick socius
When clowns themselves are neoned in
At least kids, new forms of screaming
Until another disaster gathers us

5.18

Ticked talk, picked pocket, doctor's report
A closed-up windpipe on a windowsill
Three distinctly different definitions of the dead
Noise of running in leaves, wind-jumps
Pull a bent feather from the threadbare
Where hope is the door it is stained with time
Only one nobody can play at an interval
Buildings off an on-ramp, cylindrical risers
Postage-stamp-sized historic sundowns
Any monster's larynx, any fabulous shadow
To slit speculation up its middle
Larvae revolving around the sun-star
Throat-folds unfolded, bright red threadings
Nets of meshed vessels & juicy tissues
Spread out along lengthening sunset-fingers
A material world writhing & coursing
Pulse with undergrowth, continents, axes
Articulate, viscous, multiform oneness
Mouth-parts are valleys, bronchial canyons
Our pain is how little we perceive
Nervendings in a blue-lipped stream
Embroidered dollhouse stuffed with human
Meanwhile the hereafter went to seed
A field of brightness-headed, rain-crowned
Impossible lives passed through a chair
Wooden picture, tall frame, living air

5.18

Room dim, noise of window fan
Candle in far corner, a suggestion
Little flickering life in far corner
Implication of presence of mind
Something to use the air at least
Faint red light from sign in street
The average dark green now nighttime
Old story, still stirrings, tracery
To see dust-motes collecting however
This is not a nighttime pastime
Very few seasons to a room maybe
Wide floorboards, shadow-angles, seen
Reality somehow dimmer than
Find a loophole in the paintchips
Lost postulates, bracelet of bright
The sleepers' vehicles day-await them
To slip into that body, rubber & glass
Intersections, eagerly, numb, open
Be sure to polish all your lenses
The cranium waits, quiet in corners
Something gutters, rainspouts, drains
Neat bisection of room & air
An equation of tiniest droplets
As tongue touches its mouth-roof
Somewhere must be infinite fingers

5.19

What the tongue's dying to
In the first place
External world within
Sense has three reasons
Microseconds membranous
Brainwaves in a whirlwind
In that thirst place dizzies
A ladder has quick symptoms
Gravity platonic unhurried
Nervous sons & daughters of
The flight-suit the hemisphere
Organs sprout from ground
Lips dry around when
Bent on resembles
An atmosphere of eventual
The rector had a seizure
Foresight stumbled, thunder
Whereas flesh & blood played
In lost places spasms
Across sonorous hollows
Day all grown up thrives
Settlements of weedy rust
A structural thirst
Now have a go at what
Guttural aching noise
Clear grey rain arrives
So that

5.19

To move through useless
Any fold of sudden
A purpose of air or
Breathing detail
Old machine, cloud cover
There is really so little
Flight above ground
Inbetweens, weed-gaps
Steady undulant cumulus
A rainbarrel was care
Collections shiny instants
All cats are strays
We came crying hither
And then foreclosure
Bodies enclosed in debt
Suffocation-persons
Time gets longer slower
Shelter of lonely others
Or fill a head with garbage
Unrecognizable later
Wandering under selves
What cried to be born

5.25

Any scene of shelter, of temporary
Other accompaniments, procedurals
Grass woven over our round heads
Hovering, humanoid cloud masses
Stories made of skin & eyes, a yes
Three or four infant teeth extruding
Yet the wind gentles, wavering
Greenskinned pond behind parking lot
You threw pieces of the scene in
Lost cat's collar, some runner's shoe
A human amalgam awaited trains
Weather could not be pawned off on such
Rain-dotted eggs suspended in air
The X-rays inconclusive, open-throated
Small far voice from near corner
They digitized her marrow a surprise
A kingdom of bright lichen, complexities
If only to go warm is gorgeous
Your entrails followed suit intact
We were pursued by rubber persons
Beneath the ruins were corporate structures
Some of these appendages are eternal
A cluster of spectres may curtail you
Given the pleasures of redolent night
So put the corpse beneath the couch
Your turn to turn the lever on the light

5.28

A slightly more open enclosure
Cool air stillness pools
All possible longing
The whys & wherefores of whens
Letters of glass, passages
Hold tight to flightpaths
Mouth a means of excursus
Limbs more articulate slightly
What the subject
Avenue in any rain warm
Signs are thinking
Crows, telephone polarity
Feathers are not apparel
An edge of the metal table
Where is porous, listens
Or on all fours
Skin slick with what
Seasons easy abstractions
Not Caterpiller nor Fly
A mystery treed
Thrown on a lawn
Mind before dawn
As echoes nearer
Wonder of thumb & forefinger
Aboveground freedoms slightly
Microchanges in crowfeathers
A warmth of oncoming
Moisture's impersonal kiss

5.28

Situated human thing
Aggregations of echoes
Doing things to grammar
Transparency, summers
Curvaceous daylight
Sculpture of air
Bedecked rainy diadem
Attention spans fluid
A moist distance reddens
Beyond that this
All thisness
Thistles, named faces
Significance harps
Roger that
Isolate flecks
Green thought speckled
Sutured universal
Beginning ending
A pointed sentence
Ants on the counter
Pigeons have poise
Something predating song
Instruments of bone
Matter for another
World begets world
Inklings of blue
Beyond another end

6.13

Predawn hum, open, empty-filled
A nonconsideration of movement
Bird-assemblies already begun
Before a daily world returns
These fuses noise a music
A million tongues moistening
So why a hollow room where human
Foam of pattern, whorled ears
Some clothed dust in dark blue chair
A language-precipitate extruded
Tongue & teeth older than speech
Young boy barking from a sycamore
For muddy forms still huddled
Generations of spasms of signs
Wonder wanted to tell a story
The comings closer stumbling away
Broad tall clouds of summer storm
All the lost little additions to the picture
The nothing-voiced, now-here guttering
To exist as uncertainties physiological
Outside loud bright-lit carnival
For whom & how a home
Upturned notions in sections of soil
If one could only stay awhile
Where dark & light & time & air
As matter moistens its lips

[AFTERWORD, BY KARL PARKER]

1.25.17

Human Abstract was begun—unbeknownst to me—two winters ago, in the midst of a felt deadness, where I could not write and had not written in many months, & felt somewhat desperate. I decided I wasn't going to write or try to write poetry, which for me had always meant concatenated sentences of a kind of I, a persona-speaker however lineated. Now I would just write fragments, or mutters, or fits & starts of whatever sort. That early January I wrote such, down the empty-looking page of my sketchbook. I had to do something; these at least, and *as* leasts, were something. "A tree tossed on a lawn" was the phrase that occurred to me as I stood on my upstairs porch briefly breathing & seeing a former-Christmas pine on its side just off the neighbors' opposite sidewalk. I thought, wait, Ok, I'll go back in & start there, & did. I didn't start to return to this nightly 'til I did, 'til it had started to gather its own strange momentum. The first ten or so are just moving in this new space, not all fragmentary, but by "Privacy, exhalations, quiet," a kind of way of moving in this new nightspace had been self-established: I felt a space for me opening up, returnable-to, usually beginning around three in the morning, & thence toward dawn; a whole hemisphere mostly asleep; this strange freedom in privacy, & because it's not like I "knew" what I was doing, by that time I just had to and wanted to and would keep returning. Usually, during that period, two or three written a night. It felt to me like writing ex nihilo, or rather, from the nothing of this nonetheless perceptible betweenspace, & any fragments or phrases that would occur—not toward any specific poetic telos. They seemed to be arrangements with a kind of flow that would end somewhere before pagebottom. As I said, through February and After, I wasn't thinking about them, just returning & enjoying returning & producing whatever these things were, in their patchworks of isolations, since they're, as single phrases or units, able to jump from one thing to another, I was not creating wholes, or if they are, they are discontinuous wholes bound by time & space; thus the dates as titles; time was & is the frame. The strangest thing I have to say about this time of writing is probably the only thing I shouldn't say to someone else; not just because it was the most private strange thing I've ever experienced in my life, certainly in my writing life; this is the first time I've ever tried to write it; during these nightly inbetweenspace returnings, while sitting in the very same chair by a dirty nightwindow as I am now, as I was writing I could feel the presence of two vibrating membranes (the only words I can think of for this/them), I could feel them at the sides of the space where I was writing, almost or practically in the air, just sort of quivering there, like if you put your two arms out with palms inward, the parentheses of this space—but again, I felt them there night after night and would sometimes just remember, wow, yes, *those*, during the day, but I was not thinking about them; some space of creation had opened up, I say now, & I could return to it night after night; I would go to bed near dawn (not, anyway, unusual hours for me in recent years) with a feeling of happiness in my body sometimes remembering particular things I'd written, but mostly there was just this suffused Sense that something was happening; and of course, my proceedings were also proceeding toward Spring; my winters very very hard often have been; we would proceed toward Spring, and those beautiful presences just sort of gently vibrating, but membranes, not abstract "presences" at all. Not even beautiful. Unreal, real? *There*. And that's all I think I'll ever say about that, in writing or otherwise. But the range & dexterity of the pieces was growing, & I felt actual delight in my body. The first book, about 84 pp. in this kind of layout, is Winter; the second, 60-something, is Spring; the third is the next year, much more sporadically, Winter to Spring/Summer, beginning earlier and ending later, but by that time—I can't tell you how it feels to say this—the membranes had gone, the rhythm of the whole process different, and I wasn't even sure if I wasn't just continuing on in a mode, or a sense of a time of creation, that had played itself out, so sometimes I was forcing myself either to write "regular" kinds of poems, or just not to write, not to show up if what had been was gone. Only when I looked back and started—it took me nearly a year to even look at them—to type them up did I realize that they were quite different voices that add something to what I thought was The Book (one Winter to Spring); hard for me to characterize, & pointless, really, but, in a way, to have another year experienced in this mode adds a further temporal overlay of voices to the first two modes. In every case, the three (the Third is also 60-something) Are the Book. Though there's sometimes humor & phantasmagoria, there are sometimes cries of suffering & outrage, the registration of temperatures & weather, the palpable sense of a human being continuing (merely continuing) in time; there are a multitude of references, sometimes torqued or wobbled or truncated or prostheticized, to the poetry that is part of the very fabric of my being & the fabric of this & the last two centuries or more; there are celebrations of the rebirth of organic life & sunlight & warm rain; there is ongoing & a music of utterance, at times obsessive & mutated, discontinuous wholes in time, & they are aching to be read, & understood as aggregates, within each & as an entirety. Each part reflects the whole, & the whole each part, the fractalized lyric/ post-lyric maybe, at this point no one knows (two years of having them rejected by some version of everyone). I do know, however—in all humility I say—they truly slowly teach someone how to read them, & that what they do is important to American poetry & human being in our time.

HUMAN ABSTRACT JOURNAL

Privacy, exhalation, night.

Deep in it, a sleeping hemisphere.

The head bends, curves toward.

Fingerings, textures, a quiet hum.

Aren't we folded into it, no matter what.

Maybe meaningless statements

Or a gesture, a twitch, a touched page.

These signs neither crude nor elegant.

Half things - as - they - were, half ghost.

Time is in the nightmare, soundless

scream, someone screaming without sound.

But this business was infinite

a little tear in the fabric of the everything
looked through, like the center of that scream.

So night's a throat, no wonder dark

Just up and under down, swallows

or these new titterings, uneasy,
too easy to say swallows

The will to always be bodied, why.

Dim the world w all its voices
a little, w wait

There might be slight creepings, a
small, pale tendril of thought

A gesture of a sentence as it
occurs

But there are reasons, unneeded

This candle lit for my dead friend

This little bit of ongoing in the
emptiness

Simply space w time are is meant

Streetlight glitter on the long gnarled
icicles hanging from a neighbor's roof

This was then, a quiet then, dim

Merely to hear w have the last
almost-nothing sounds

A woman day, distant flickers

And the city glitters w breathes from
signals, blinks, a column of steam a crevice

By the time you get these notes + messages
Beyond the hood is blue then black
Insects swarm the light certain seasons
Wind a warm muzzle, redundance
The child you were in there
That one changed continuity
Mouths of eyes, leaf-fallings, flares
An old ache a young nothing touches
Interstate through grassy backyards
Once-beloved stuffed animals buried
Quiet roar of days in the ear
That time when, how you, and then
Still the accumulations of bodily shock
Waves of feeling, mostly mute, fallings
Those buildings down
Rolling clouds of ash, papers swirling
Everyday bright blue beginning day
That time when, how you, and then
History in retrospect fractalized
The Mouths aswarm, with the tickling writhes
A tongue to lick that clock
Cloth arm from a pocket taken

Ache a minute for that one gone
Hands usually up to something
Scrawled note, no secret
Same ache over time
Only layered as skin regrows
Splayed breathing inside secret
all know the loved one goes
The eyes hair smell of him or her
The touch of, Feel of
Slow long shock of really gone
No more to be met with
Changes the whole landscape
As if blood-ache in a sunset
Well-worn paths these meanings
As if nothing-ache in a nowhere
Bright snow almost not even falling
This was the season of this as ever
Will have been a torso's arms reaching
And touch the thing thinking of
To touch again a warm second
Is all the ache says, pulses, tonight

A sentence, a lifetime, roadside snowbank
Insistent rhythmic arrival, thuds
Beneath these cities waterways, catacombs
In a hollow glass globe spiders spin
Tossed corn, flicker-shines, one wish
That time you held a shoot in your hand
A thousand years and more
Removal - figure formed of snow
Knowledge wrapped in old wool blankets
Somebody shed an outcropping, sudden
Caverned canyons in those eyes
A penny for the quietest thoughts
Flickers in the cupboard under the sink
Smell of stain remover, weak bleach
Occasionally angry neighbors stagger, stare
To have walked 20 highway miles that day
One set of summer mountains one after another
people passing in the creek looked
Childhood looked, cloudy puffy somethings
Why continually return to sky
If the eye were an animal, its soul
Naturally not predicated on permanence
No doubt those hummingbirds, that hill
All eyes at last closed, but not yours

Cat, moon, metal screen, ~~pleasure dome~~.
no nearer.

otherwheres
Thoughts of others now to one side put.

As if a shine, hiding, in a head of hair.

snuffed
Or = Extinguished candle, impressions, ~~hard~~ cold wax.

leaf-flutter, cloud-wisps, neon hums.

late
Wonders done down one last street.

Blinks and something lightly biting skin.

To feel the cool small sharp real teeth of.

Signs and wonder-signs, worlds advertised.

farther
Another cat, ~~matter~~ moon, X-rays free.

Mutters, where was the, that again.

weirdly,
Keys are close at hand, easy as knees.

Any puddle trembles container reflective.

And the rest of those animals hidden, true.

No-one did it stumble ever, a blue ear.

Objects in mirror are nearer in reverse, no

Hanging like an oasis in a wet desert.

somewhere   bright
Shimmers later, little [Illusory] bite-points.

Torn moon, screen clawed in, curled form.

Stories were always, were anyway old.
Something about the tilty deck of a ship.
Or transcendence, cosmonauts, the like.
The root of the moon, antagonisms, ilks.
We were followed by a pleasant monster.
We were robots, we didn't care.
By the end something momentous had been.
The tide went in + out, geosynchronicity.
Narcolepsy found its way into thick novels.
A sestina was arrested for malingering.
Everyone knows exactly what this means.
The wall is on the writing, always was.
Eternity will steal your best ideas.
So put the butcher knife back OK.
If your hair is long + blue you are blessèd.
Your turn inside the prism's coming soon.
We are incapable of not dreaming this now.
And again when you return somehow.
Graining image of fireworks, sound turned down.
Grainy flickering amazement too, at you.

Heat a result of ~~motion~~ vibration, kinesis

Body of sunlight, body of god

The season's flies as yet unborn

Fool-king + shepherdess or ~~Mad~~ ~~Queen~~ Mad Queen

Queen mabye, ~~webs of~~ dewdropped webs,

Spiderglitters across down-grass

Spread out ointments please

Collections for spreading breathing

A vial of tears around a neck

Space-time slightly different there

Enveloping neck + its outpourings

Vertebrae in a ~~tissued~~ layered prism

Our histories those of ~~atoms~~ electrons observed

Small striped cat sleeps in a window

Stripes + his smile sleep

None of this predictably changed

A language of exile + return

Another life held in a hand

These raps may be read through

Organism-squirm, outposts, pasts

Between upheavals for the nonce

Something gentle, massive, swims the air

First sounds, dawn-birds, beginnings
Come + go now, images of the gone
Continual movements matterial forms
One is one awhile among others
A face cannot be ~~captured~~ rendered in an image
A kind of gaping aching tenderness at
What your face says when no-one sees   times
Gorgeous redundancies of warm rain
Night-drops, soon blue dawn
Vehicle-sounds, workday doings
Bloodstreams, quotas, interpersonal chemistries
Our charts suggest spastic developments
The plot congeals, the atmosphere an engine
Bones of contention in the throat of things
Yet a kind of smile hidden in air
Sunlight is not an arm of fire
The bones of the face opening at last
Bird-flight, flickerings, scatters, patterns
Ground surging with worm-activity
The first few cars, red taillights, slowly
                                          thinking,
Again a human day, thisness, ~~the~~ blue
                              electric

Neither dark nor light, no answer
Night however within without
We move along among surfaces
Throat-song in a far corner
Or some kid playing with time
Removals, new uses, stretched youth
Butterflies raised behind bay windows
The glass of a face, self-portraiture)
Parts of ourselves gone then
A chatter of culture, smeared lens
Azure hath a conker
Daily evening recital [of] violence
The assailant wore a face or faces
Points of view [for] ~~hurried eyes~~ reshuffled by
Amid a thousand blind windows
What matter who speaks
These are the days that were her eyes
And by no man these verses
Neither from nor toward, no wonder
~~That way moves, slash marks~~
Thisness, winter stasis, embers
Deep quiet between night & day
~~Cold~~ FROZEN musics, bodies gone ~~dumb~~
The boy with blue teeth (~~still~~) laughs
There was a world, it had a moon

ACKNOWLEDGEMENTS

The posthumous publication of this book presented a special set of complications that could have easily halted the project but for the efforts of a small cluster of people who remained devoted to Karl's work. There's no doubt he'd have wanted to thank those who made it possible.

Enormous gratitude to everyone at Threadsuns Press: to Michael Flatt for believing in this book, and to Erica Johnson, Nicole Prince, and Julianne Kendrick for your creative vision, labor, and attention to detail throughout the publication process.

Sincere appreciation to the Parker family for granting permissions to the work.

A collection of 27 poems and the preface to this book appeared in *Stone Canoe*, no. 15 (2021) thanks to the generosity of Phil Memmer. Thanks, also, to Gillian Conoley at *VOLT* for publishing II.4.24 (vol. 22, 2017). Karl got to see that one in print.

Warmest thanks to Fanny Howe, Alice Fulton, and CAConrad, for your enthusiastic support for the book.

To Karen Leona Anderson, Bill Petit, Jon Schmitt, Reb Livingston, Sarah Ahrens, and Megan Davidson: your enduring friendship helped to nurture and sustain the mind that produced these poems.

And to Roger Gilbert, Tim Carter, and Gabe Gudding, for your encouragement, insight, perspective, and camaraderie in refusing to let this work go unseen: *thank you*.

KARL PARKER'S first book of poems, *Personationskin*, was published by No Tell Books in 2009. For over 20 years, he taught poetry and creative writing at universities and other institutions across the state of New York. He died in 2019, leaving behind several unpublished manuscripts, including *Human Abstract*.